HEROES OF KETTLE CREEK

Also by Christine R. Swager:

Black Crows and White Cockades
If Ever Your Country Needs You
Come to the Cow Pens!
The Valiant Died: The Battle of Eutaw Springs

HEROES OF KETTLE CREEK

1779-1782

By

Christine R. Swager

Maps by:
Steven Rauch and John Robertson

ISBN 0-7414-5040-2

Published by:

INFIN∩ITY
PUBLISHING.COM

1094 New DeHaven Street, Suite 100
West Conshohocken, PA 19428-2713
Info@buybooksontheweb.com
www.buybooksontheweb.com
Toll-free (877) BUY BOOK
Local Phone (610) 941-9999
Fax (610) 941-9959

Printed in the United States of America

Printed on Recycled Paper

Published October 2008

CONTENTS

PREFACE

State histories usually limit their content to events which occur within the confines of the state lines. Although this may be expedient, the result may overlook significant events. This is the case in Georgia history of the Revolutionary War.

The British occupation of the South began in Georgia and the early Georgia events are significant. However, when Georgia was conquered, and was returned to the status of royal colony, what did the Georgia Patriots do? Did they hunker down and wait out the events of the war? Certainly not.

The Georgia Patriots moved out of their state and confronted the enemy in North and South Carolina. They participated in almost every battle which was fought in the western Carolinas. They took a decisive role at Fort Thicketty, Wofford's Ironworks, Musgrove's Mill, Blackstock's and many others. When the two most important American victories in the south were fought at King's Mountain and Cowpens, the Georgians were there.

The Georgia Society, Sons of the American Revolution has researched many of the Georgians of the Revolutionary period and documented their contributions. Few are remembered today. It was not always so. Fifty-nine of the counties in Georgia were named for participants in the American Revolution. It is time their deeds were revisited.

This is not a history text. It is a story of the men and women who distinguished themselves at a time when their opposition to the British could mean death. It is the story of how and why those few Georgia Patriots became involved in the backcountry battles in Georgia and the Carolinas.

This story cannot relate every incidence of bravery, every small militia group: there were many. It focuses on the Wilkes County Militia, the Georgia unit which participated in the Patriot victory over the enemy at the Battle of Kettle Creek. Certainly, we will encounter other groups as they move in and out of the picture, but the heroes of Kettle Creek are typical of the Georgians who carried on the resistance even when their own state was occupied by the enemy. It is their story which is told here.

Although this is not a text book, references are cited so the reader can read further. History is a story and the story of the Georgians and other southern Patriots in the Revolution is one which should excite the imagination and engender pride in their accomplishments. This book, hopefully, will stimulate the reader to search further for the exploits of the Georgia militia in general and the heroes of Kettle Creek in particular.

ACKNOWLEDGMENTS

I am indebted to the Georgia Society, Sons of the American Revolution for inviting me to Kettle Creek and introducing me to the heroes who fought there. Who could resist the drama of such a battle and the militia leaders who fought so heroically?

Any storyteller must depend on the research of serious scholars, and I have been fortunate in having the help of the finest. Robert Scott Davis, who is the premier writer on Kettle Creek and its participants, shared his body of writing with me. He forwarded material, published and unpublished, which related to my topic. I am grateful for his generosity.

Steven Rauch, Military Historian at Fort Gordon, Georgia, has prepared maps on the battle which are included in this test. His work on the monument is included as Appendix I. His articles on the two battles of Augusta provide valuable insight into those events, and into the motivations of the people involved. Steve took time from his own writing to review the manuscript and made valuable corrections and suggestions, as well as writing the Introduction. His friendship and kindness are greatly appreciated.

The late Dr. Edward Cashin's work provides a complete study of Lt. Col. Thomas Brown, a villain of the story, and his career as a Loyalist officer. Lawrence Babits's work on the Battle of Cowpens, **A Devil of a Whipping,** and John Buchanan's **Road to Guilford Courthouse**, cover that battle and the harrowing trek across North Carolina in which the Georgians participated.

Patrick O'Kelley's monumental four-volume **Nothing but Blood and Slaughter** allowed me to trace the Georgians involved in the conflicts across the south. I am indebted to him and to all the scholars who have researched the war in the south.

Jason Baker, ranger and interpreter formerly at Fort Morris, Georgia, and now at Fort King George, reviewed the chapter on early Georgia history to be sure the content told the story accurately. Colonel George Thurman of the Georgia Society, Sons of the American Revolution, and Lillie Crowe, Librarian at the Mary Willis Library in Washington, Georgia, were kind enough to read a preliminary draft.

All lovers of history are indebted to Charles Baxley, publisher of the online **Southern Campaigns of the American Revolution (SCAR)**. He, and his colleague, David Reuher, have provided a venue for serious scholars and avocational historians to share their research. Not only has the publication focused on larger battles such as the Battle of Camden and the Battle of Eutaw Springs, but also brought attention to lesser known events such as Kettle Creek, Earle's Ford, and Beattie's Mill. Historians now have a place to share their writing about local Patriots such as Elijah Clarke, James Williams, James McCall, and John Dooly, as well as the adversaries such as Thomas Waters and William Cunningham. Those interested in Georgia history will find several articles in SCAR by Robert Scott Davis and Steven Rauch. All issues of the publication are available online at:

www.southerncampaigns.org

My long-time friend and cartographer, John Robertson, continues to provide maps to illustrate the story and provided computer assistance. His latest project involves locating the sites of Revolutionary War battles. This work, which is ongoing, is available at:

http://jrshelby.com/sc-links/gaz/index.htm

Every weekend hundreds of men, women and children leave behind the comforts of the twenty-first century to participate in Revolutionary War encampments, battle reenactments and living history tableaus. They endeavor to accurately portray uniforms, clothing, utensils, weapons and manners of the Revolutionary War period. Over the years they have provided thousands of spectators and encampment visitors with the experience of what it was like to live and to fight in the Revolutionary War. I appreciate the dedication and contributions of all reenactors, and especially those who posed, in character, for this book.

My fellow Revolutionary War enthusiasts have been most generous and I appreciate their help and interest in my project. A new friend, Dwight Ellisor, an artist of considerable talent, drew the sketches. Will Graves, a friend of long standing, not only provided the photo of the James McCall reenactor on horseback, but also forwarded a copy of the pension application of Jesse Gordon, a member of the Wilkes County Militia. Gordon fought at Carr's Fort, Kettle Creek and Augusta where he was taken prisoner and interned at Fort Cornwallis. That account provided me with an appreciation of what these men suffered.

Finally, my husband has accompanied me on this journey into Georgia's Revolutionary history. It was a project I could not have undertaken without his help.

Christine R. Swager
Moore, South Carolina
August 2008

INTRODUCTION

My dear friend Dr. Christine Swager has become one of the most prolific authors about the Revolutionary War in the South. I first met Chris about five years ago at an obscure revolutionary war battlefield which then was not even on the official state map of Georgia. That battlefield was Kettle Creek, near Washington, Georgia, a site which forms the nucleus of this book. I was giving a battlefield tour on the terrain as part of the annual Georgia Society, Sons of the American Revolution (GASSAR) commemoration of the battle held every February. The terrain at Kettle Creek is not the most easy to walk, with dense underbrush and sharp contours. Yet there was Chris, a retired professor from the University of South Carolina, out in the cold weather and walking the damp ground determined to understand first hand the nature of the land where Americans, both patriot and loyalist, fought and died over 225 years ago. Oh, and the fact that she has had knee replacement surgery did not deter her quest for knowledge on that uneven terrain. Chris Swager is a determined woman who does not hesitate to tell anyone she meets that her mission in this phase of her life is to push back the frontiers of ignorance of our society through education about the events of the American Revolution.

Though Chris claims not to be a historian, the book you are reading about Georgia's role in the Revolution is based upon research in primary and secondary sources of history. Chris has drawn upon a wide variety of sources to tell this story about the Georgia heroes of Kettle Creek and other battles. She has walked the battlefields, read the diaries and pension statements, consulted historians, historical reenactors, and anyone else who might provide some insight into the actions of that time. Chris and I regularly attend Revolutionary War roundtables and battlefield discovery trips as part of an informal organization called the Southern Campaigns of the American Revolution, or SCAR as it is more affectionately known. Through SCAR's efforts to promote the preservation, study, and commemoration of both the famous and obscure battles of the Revolution, much progress has been made in recognizing Georgia as the often "forgotten front" of the southern campaign. Chris has taken the knowledge gained from SCAR and her research to write this book to shine much needed light upon those Georgians whose lives should be remembered by succeeding generations.

This book tells the story of men and women such as Elijah Clarke, John Dooly, William Few, and Nancy Hart whose names are still with us in Georgia today marking counties, parks and buildings. In Columbia County, Georgia, where I live, the William Few Parkway is named for one of the most dedicated patriots from the war. With the publication of this book, the deeds of men such as Few will be accessible to a wider audience. Chris has written this book mainly for young people, to be used in schools, youth organizations and libraries to help educate readers about these Georgia heroes. Hers is a noble effort for which she deserves our most sincere thanks as Georgians and Americans. Someone else who deserves our thanks is Bob Swager, Chris's husband and a retired US Army Chaplain, who has been her dedicated assistant throughout this effort. Both Bob and Chris could have just retired to an easy, quiet life but instead chose to embark upon this crusade of which this book is tangible evidence of their appreciation for those Georgia heroes of battles such as Kettle Creek.

Steven J. Rauch
US Army Historian
Evans, Georgia
August 2008

HEROES OF KETTLE CREEK

Early Georgia—Chapter 1

In 1663, the Carolina Charter gave to the Lords Proprietors territory from 36° 30″ to the 29th parallel. The northern border of this new territory was Virginia and the southern border extended to St. Augustine, Florida. All the land from the Atlantic Ocean westward was covered by the charter and that included what is now Georgia. Therefore, early Georgia history is the story of the Carolina settlement.

The intention of the holders of the Carolina Charter was to make money. One of the first profitable ventures was trading with the Indians for deer skins and furs. With a demand for leather in Europe, the deer skins were highly prized. In the area which would become Georgia, game was plentiful and the Indian inhabitants were accustomed to trading. In addition to deer, buffalo herds roamed the area. Fur-bearing animals such as beaver, fox, mink, otter, and bear were abundant. The territory could provide any type of leather or fur which fashion-conscious Europeans desired.

However, the interest in this bounty was not limited to the English who occupied the area around Charleston. The Spanish who occupied Florida at that time, and the French who had moved down the Mississippi River from Canada, coveted the wealth in skins. Conflicts with those nations, and the Indians which they enlisted, made the back-country hazardous. Also, unscrupulous traders often cheated the Indians. The Indians, in retaliation, attacked settlers and the few settlers in the back country were often driven out.

Illustration by Dwight Ellisor.

The colonists in South Carolina who settled along the coast found rice and indigo to be profitable; however, these labor-intensive crops required large plantations supported by slave labor. As the numbers of slaves in Carolina grew, this added another threat to life in the low country. The possibility of slave revolts intensified the anxiety of the citizens.

Spain offered sanctuary to any slave who escaped to the Florida territory. To attempt to counter the threat of both the Spanish and French, the British had constructed Fort King George on the Altamaha River. (Spaulding, 1991:15). Still, the threats from Spain and France and the Indian unrest, along with the possibility of any of these enemies combining their efforts, haunted the Carolina rice barons.

The citizens of South Carolina petitioned England to establish a royal colony which would act as a buffer between the plantation society and the Indian, the Spanish and the French threats. In June of 1732, a charter was granted which would establish a new colony between the Savannah and Altamaha Rivers and, north of the source of these rivers, extend to the Mississippi River. The colony would be named Georgia after the reigning monarch, King George II.

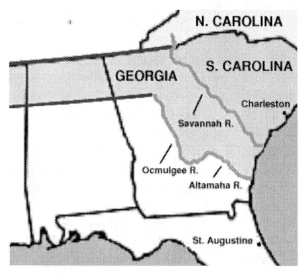

Georgia Colony Established in 1732

Although England set aside the territory as a new colony, the area was already inhabited. For generations Cherokee and Creek Indians had made this their home. There were Indian towns in the area, and the Indians grew crops and hunted the wild game. They dealt with the white men who came for the fur trade which was profitable. However, the native peoples would not relinquish their land willingly. There would be trouble to come.

Georgia was a noble experiment. The Carolinians saw the colony as merely a buffer between themselves and the dangers they faced: the King saw other possibilities. Because of economic conditions in England, many men were unemployed and faced debtors' prison. The King reasoned that many of these were men of good character who, through no fault of their own, would always be in dire circumstances. A colony populated with these men would allow them to prosper and they would be highly motivated to succeed when this opportunity presented itself. It is probable that this approach was influenced by General James Edward Oglethorpe, a member of parliament, who had exposed the wretched conditions of the prisons. Oglethorpe had advocated that many of these men could find success in new colonies in North America.

Also, Georgia would provide a safe haven for European Protestants who suffered from religious persecution. (Spaulding, 1991:17).

The vision was that a colony based on silk would prosper. The mulberry trees, upon which this industry depended, would grow in Georgia's climate and provide success for those willing to labor. Settlers in Georgia would profit from the colony and protect their own livelihood as well as that of the Carolinians.

In July of 1732, General Oglethorpe was selected to accompany the new colonists and establish the new settlement. It was a wise choice. Not only did Oglethorpe agree with the mission of the colony but he was an experienced soldier who could provide protection for the colonists.

The ship *Anne* sailed for the New World on 16 November 1732 with 114 colonists aboard. The colonists had been carefully chosen and limited to those of good character, and men with skills which could benefit the colony. The suggestion that Georgia was inhabited by debtors from prison is unfounded. (Coleman, 1978:2). Only settlers who would benefit the colony were selected from the applicants.

The ship arrived in Charleston, South Carolina, on 13 January 1733. The South Carolinians, cognizant of the security these new colonists would provide, greeted them warmly and donated 104 head of breeding cattle, 25 hogs and 20 barrels of rice. These gifts were loaded into local boats and accompanied by rangers to protect the cargo, as well as the new arrivals, from any mishaps. (McCall, 1909:21).

On 12 February 1733 Oglethorpe landed at Yamacraw Bluff which he selected as the town site. The bluff overlooked a navigable river, and he chose to name the new settlement after the river: Savannah. The city was laid out in squares which still characterize the city today.

A portion of an early map of Savannah by Jones.

James Oglethorpe was a visionary, but he was also very practical. He realized that Georgia would not profit from a society such as that of South Carolina. On the coast of Carolina large rice plantations operated with slave labor. Tremendous acreages had few armed men who could protect the colony in case of slave revolts, Indian attacks or an invasion by the Spanish. Oglethorpe envisioned Georgia as a colony of yeomen farmers, each with small holdings. This concentration of population would provide militia, citizen soldiers, for the defense of the colony.

In the early colonial period, all white men thirteen or older were required to participate in the defense of the colony. They mustered, or assembled, periodically to train and, when danger threatened, they came together to fight the enemy. The militia chose their own leaders who were usually men who were prominent in the colony. Oglethorpe saw the need for a strong militia which farmers with small holdings would provide. It was for this reason that slavery was prohibited in early Georgia. Time and events would prove that Oglethorpe was correct.

The colonization of Georgia was vigorously promoted and one hundred and thirty Scots came and settled on the coast at a place they called Inverness, now modern Darien, on the Altamaha River.

Colonists settled along the rivers. Many were German Protestants who were fleeing religious persecution in Europe. Over one hundred German farmers settled at Ebenezer, a site north of the town of Savannah, on the Savannah River. Others soon joined them and a prosperous community was established.

Since, for the new colony to succeed, it needed to establish trade with the Indians, Augusta was established in 1737. (Cashin, 1996:9). It was built below the falls on the Savannah River at the head of navigation. It was an excellent location as animals had long used the rocks at the fall line of the Savannah to cross. (Cashin, 1996:3). Later Indian trails crossed the Savannah River there, and the traders used the crossing to pass from South Carolina to Georgia. Warehouses were stocked with trade goods and skins collected there could be transported by boat directly to Charleston.

Observing that trading rum with the Indians resulted in problems and, believing that the use of hard liquor resulted in poor health and disease, Oglethorpe moved to prohibit the rum trade. Further, since most of the Indian trade was centered in Georgia, he required that all traders get a license to trade in this new colony. His prohibitions were considered an affront to the Carolinians and there was considerable friction between Oglethorpe and his South Carolina neighbors.

Aware that the purpose of the Georgia colony was to counter the threat of Spain toward Carolina, Oglethorpe established forts at Savannah and Augusta. He also built a fort on St. Simon's Island on a bluff overlooking a sharp bend in the inland passage. In the days of sailing ships the bend would make it difficult for an enemy to approach without facing the guns of the fort. Oglethorpe called the new site Fort Frederica after the only son of King George II.

Spain contested the placement of Fort Frederica, contending that the territory belonged to Spain. Oglethorpe argued that, since it was north of the Altamaha, it was on Georgia territory. He also built fortifications on Jekyl Island and argued that since the St. Johns River was a tributary of the Altamaha, the Georgians could build and defend to that boundary. An examination of the map shows that not to be the case, but it does suggest that Oglethorpe was a commander of great daring. His goal was to establish a safe colony for settlement.

In September 1738, a regiment of British troops arrived in Georgia after the British Parliament saw the danger to all the colonies if Georgia were to be taken by the Spanish.

Spain continued to interfere in the affairs of the English colonies. They not only protected slaves who escaped from South Carolina, but actively recruited escaped slaves. In the fall of 1739, slaves in the Charleston area rebelled in what is known as the Stono Rebellion. It was known that the slaves intended to march to Spanish Florida and freedom. The rebellion was put down but not without bloodshed. General Oglethorpe knew that war with Spain was inevitable and prepared his little army to defend Georgia.

Eventually, Spain claimed that the Georgia territory was Spanish and prepared to go to war to enforce that claim. General Oglethorpe established his headquarters at Fort Frederica and stationed batteries on Jekyl and Cumberland Islands to counter the threat. He also established a chain of forts south to the St. Johns River.

War was declared between England and Spain in October 1739. After an unsuccessful attempt to capture St. Augustine from the Spanish in 1740, General Oglethorpe withdrew and turned his attention to securing Georgia's defenses.

In June of 1742, the Spanish fleet moved against the Georgia outposts at St. Simon's Island. Unable to defend the battery, Oglethorpe spiked the guns and withdrew to Fort Frederica. The Spanish moved against that fort by water and land but were unable to displace General Oglethorpe's troops. The campaign ended in July of 1742, when General Oglethorpe's troops inflicted heavy casualties on the Spanish in an event known as The Battle of the Bloody Marsh. Although Georgia was established to provide a buffer for South Carolina against the Spanish, South Carolina provided no troops when this threat arose. It was the Georgia militia and British troops under General Oglethorpe who won the victory over Spain.

Although most of the settlers in the colonies gave credit to General Oglethorpe for eliminating the Spanish threat, the governor of South Carolina charged that Oglethorpe had not followed orders. In McCall's History of Georgia (1909), that writer estimates that General Oglethorpe's force of 650 had repulsed a Spanish force of 5000! The incident known as Bloody Marsh had ended the Spanish threat to Georgia and the adjoining colonies. However, the year after his great victory and under severe criticism, General Oglethorpe left Georgia and never returned. Nevertheless, he continued to work for the Trustees in England to support the Georgia experiment.

Wars in Europe settled the Spanish threat as Florida became a British colony in 1748. With the threat of attack diminished, the forts which Oglethorpe had established fell into disrepair and his regiment was deactivated as soldiers claimed property and settled down. The town at Fort Frederica had been a military town, serving the needs of the forces stationed there. When the fort was abandoned the town withered and eventually died. Today the site is a National Monument and an archaeological laboratory.

With the Spanish threat diminished, the settlers in Georgia were able to turn their attention to their livelihood. Food was available as fruits and vegetables grew abundantly. Deer, bear, rabbits, and other game roamed the woods, and the rivers teemed with fish. The Indians had taught the new settlers to relish shellfish which thrived in the tidewater area. (Spaulding, 1991:89).

Lumbering became profitable and wood products such as barrels and building supplies found a ready market in the West Indies and could be traded for sugar and molasses. The port at Darien became the principal port for shipping lumber. Cattle and hogs thrived in the climate and soon cattle were so numerous that animals were branded to identify ownership. The small farmers could manage well.

Illustration by Dwight Ellisor.

However, the Georgia colony had never produced the wealth that the Trustees had expected. Olives, wine and silk were expected to thrive but had been produced in small quantities, and a market for spices had not materialized.

Speculators believed that only rice could make Georgia prosper and many agitated to end the ban on slavery. The residents of Ebenezer and Darien argued against slavery on religious grounds, but to no avail. In 1750, slavery was permitted, (Spaulding, 1991:36), and plantations were established along Georgia's tidal rivers and adjoining property. The rice culture had arrived.

The Trustees could not continue without government funds and, when their request for money was rejected in 1751, it was the end of the noble experiment. In 1752, the Trustees surrendered their charter to the government and Georgia became a royal colony.

The new royal governor faced serious concerns. Roads were needed to link the settlements. Since the evacuation of General Oglethorpe's troops, there were few soldiers to defend the territory. The militia were poorly organized and could not be counted upon to protect the settlers against Indian attacks. These concerns became the focus of the new government. However, while those issues were being addressed, settlement continued.

In 1752, a group of Congregationalists moved from South Carolina to Midway and needed a port for their products. The port town of Sunbury was established on the Medway River and soon rivaled Savannah in shipping.

In 1760, a new royal governor, James Wright, was appointed and his tenure in Georgia, which lasted as long as the British controlled the area, would be one of expansion. Wright saw that wealth in Georgia required more settlers, more land and better defenses. He understood how attractive the Indian lands were to prospective settlers. Many white settlers had already moved in along the Broad River in what was clearly Indian territory. Wright looked to the Indian lands to extend Georgia's boundaries.

The opportunity to acquire territory from the Indians came when the Cherokees and the Creeks became heavily in debt to traders. In 1773, Governor Wright assumed their debt in return for their relinquishing claim on two million (2,000,000) acres in two parcels. This would become known as the "Ceded Lands." One parcel was between the Ogeechee and Altahama rivers. The other area north of Augusta would be called Wilkes County. That Wilkes County included land that is now Lincoln, Elbert and Wilkes Counties, and most of Hart, Madison, Oglethorpe, Taliaferro, and Clarke. The Wilkes County in the Revolutionary period was this large expanse of territory north of Augusta from the Savannah River inland, and bordering on territory the Indians still held.

The land was opened for settlement in small lots as Governor Wright was concerned about security for Augusta and Savannah and wanted the greatest number of men possible to provide militia units. The settler could purchase two hundred acres (200) for himself and twenty-five (25) for each member of his household. These small holdings would provide a buffer against Indian attacks.

Most of the settlers who moved into the Ceded Lands were families which had been part of the Scots-Irish migration into the back country of America. They would have a decisive impact on Georgia which continues to this day. They brought with them their speech, music, dance, crafts, religion and language as well as their distinct Presbyterian independence.

However, more important for our story is the role they played in the American War for Independence which was soon to come. They would become the heroes of the Battle of Kettle Creek

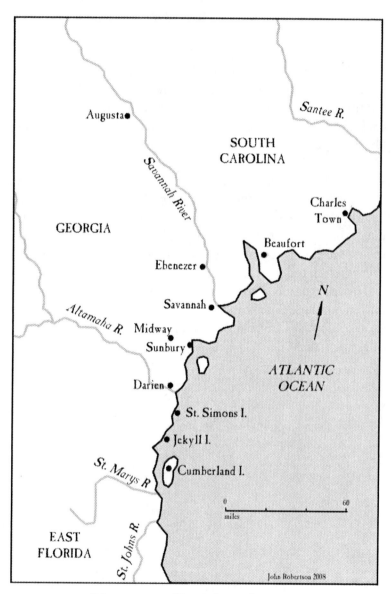

Map prepared by John Robertson

The Scots-Irish Migration—Chapter 2

The settlers we refer to as Scots-Irish (or Scotch-Irish) had a long and contentious relationship with England. Their ancestors had lived along the border between Scotland and England and had, for generations, waged war with their neighbors.

In the early 1600's, when England forced Irish chieftains from their lands, King James established what became known as the Ulster Plantation. It comprised most of what we know today as Northern Ireland. Settlers were encouraged, if not actually forced, to move into this new English territory. Many Scots and a few English families made the trip across the Irish Sea to resettle.

The Scots settled on landed estates in Ireland as renters, and established the farming practices which they had used for generations. They cleared the lands and planted crops of oats, barley, and wheat as well as vegetables for their own use. They raised cattle and sheep and supplemented their diet with dairy products and occasional meat.

For generations the Scots had been weavers. They raised sheep to provide the wool for their material. They had also learned how to separate the fibers in flax to make linen. However, when they attempted to sell their woolen and linen materials, they were considered competitors to the merchants in England who complained to the British government. Taxes and import duties were imposed on Irish goods and these restrictions prevented the Scots in Ireland from receiving fair prices for their products. (Rouse, 1995:29). Further, they were prevented by English law from trading with any other country.

England had pretended that the purpose of moving the Scots to Ireland was to have a gentling influence on 'the wild Irish tribes.' This was certainly just an excuse as the Scots were devout Presbyterians and the Irish were Roman Catholics. Because of those religious differences and cultural differences, the two groups did not intermingle. Although many Scots would be born in Ireland, and therefore referred to as 'Scots-Irish,' they would retain their Scot culture.

The Scots resided in Ireland for generations in spite of the hardships. English laws discriminated against them. Their products were taxed, their rents for the homes kept rising and they were forbidden to hold public office, enter the professions, acquire higher education, or serve in the military. All avenues of success were closed to them, but they survived in what must have been a hostile environment.

Certainly the hostility of their neighbors and of the British government forced the Scots to become more defensive as they faced enemies on all sides. As Presbyterians they believed in human equality which put them in conflict with the class system, especially with the elite landed gentry in Ireland from whom they rented property. Also, the Presbyterians believed in individualism in religious matters and accepted no authoritarian religious hierarchy. This put them in conflict with both the Roman Catholic Church and the Church of England beliefs. (Blethen & Wood, 1998:17). The fiercely independent Scots found their safety and security in their faith and their pastors provided leadership in their lives.

Finally, it would be religious persecution which would compel them to act. England had an established church, the Church of England, which was supported by the government. Every citizen in Ireland had to pay a tithe (one tenth of their income) to support the Church of England. Still, that church, jealous of its position, was determined to eliminate competition from any other religious group. About 1700, the Church of England determined to crush all opposition. To do this they needed to discredit all religious beliefs which did not support their authority. In other words, they wanted to eliminate dissenters. The Scots in Ireland were Presbyterians who challenged the authority of the Church of England and were, therefore, dissenters.

The government of England, in support of its established church, declared that all sacraments not administered by a communicant of the Church of England would be null and void. That meant that marriages, baptisms, burials and communions performed by the Presbyterian clergy were not valid. Presbyterian marriages would be illegal and the children born of those marriages would be illegitimate. Pastors who defied the law and attempted to serve their congregations were subject to arrest and imprisonment. This affront to the devout Presbyterians of Ireland forced them to take action to preserve their religious beliefs. In the early 1700's, a quarter of a million (250,000) left Ireland. (Leyburn, 1962:176). Many left as families but some Presbyterian pastors led their entire congregations out of Ireland and emigrated to America.

Although the exodus started in the early 1700's, the Presbyterians from Ireland were still arriving up till the time of the Revolutionary War when the British interfered with shipping. As late as 1772, Pastor William Martin led five shiploads of Presbyterians from Ireland to South Carolina and the settlers fanned out in the north-western part of the colony. (Scoggins, 2001:30).

America had been a haven for many who were fleeing from religious persecution. Although some colonies like South Carolina had been established with riches in mind, Europeans who were fleeing religious persecution were welcome. Most European countries had a government supported church which gave legitimacy to the government in exchange for preferential legislation. Those who did not belong to the established church were often persecuted. The Scots were persecuted economically and theologically. Some religious 'dissenters' in other countries were tortured and killed.

The earliest colonists, the Pilgrims, who landed in Plymouth in 1620, were Puritans who had been persecuted in

Europe. Others followed: Quakers who came to Pennsylvania in the 1760's had been persecuted by orthodox religions; Huguenots who were Protestant were persecuted by the French government supporting the Roman Catholic Church; Palatine Germans who were Lutheran were persecuted by their government supporting the Roman Catholic Church; Roman Catholics who were persecuted by Protestant governments settled in Maryland; Moravians, Amish, and many others had been persecuted by those who did not value their teachings. America had communities of settlers from many areas of Europe who had found religious freedom in the New World. Now the Scots would seek the same.

The Scots left Ireland from the port of Ulster on a voyage which must have been frightening in spite of its necessity. The voyage would take six weeks to ten weeks and it would be crowded and uncomfortable as well as dangerous. Many of those wishing to leave had little or no money and the passage was expensive. It is estimated that as many as one hundred thousand (100,000) of them would arrive as indentured servants.

One who could not afford the passage would negotiate with an agent to have his or her service sold in the New World in exchange for passage. When the ship arrived in port, merchants, tradesmen, farmers, householders, and others who needed help, would buy the contract from the agents. The term of service might extend from four to seven years and the contracts were enforced by the colonial officials. The servant would be housed, clothed and fed for the duration of his or her service. Upon completion of the contract the servant often was assured tools, clothing, and perhaps some other sort of recompense. (Leyburn, 1962:177).

The Scots were not the only immigrants who came to this country as indentured servants. It was common practice for those who could not afford the fare. Those were people the gentry at the time would have referred to as 'the lower orders.' (Leyburn, 1962: 177). The bulk of the immigrants to American came from 'the lower orders.'

Certainly there were abuses but, for the most part, the indenture system worked well. America was a thriving nation and needed laborers. Some servants were engaged in manual labor at farms, but others were indentured to tanners, pewterers, silversmiths, coopers (barrel makers), framers (builders) or millers. This service was similar to an apprenticeship since the servant would learn a trade which would provide him with skills to make his own way in the world when his service was complete. Similarly, young women who served with weavers, milliners (hat makers), dressmakers or other artisans, would have skills which were valuable to them.

Once their service was completed, the young Scots could have stayed in the area where they had made friends or connections, or they were free to migrate south towards the settlements where their kinsmen had stopped.

Those who came to America without indentured obligations found themselves in ports like Philadelphia which were heavily populated and expensive. The Scots tended to be rural people and these urban areas did not appeal to them. Further, with very limited resources, they could not afford the land which was available. Therefore, they moved westward through rich fertile farmland which was occupied by Germans, an area we now call Pennsylvania Dutch territory.

Finally they reached the Allegany Mountains, the boundary line of the Indian Territory which England had pledged to preserve. The pioneers turned south and followed a trail which the Indians had used for generations. The trail was originally a footpath but was later used by drovers as they herded cattle from the back country to Philadelphia. As hundreds moved down the trail, first by foot, then by horse, oxen, carts, and wagons, the trail widened and became known as the Great Wagon Road. (Rouse, 1995).

Some of the immigrants settled in western Virginia; others moved on to western North Carolina. Their holdings

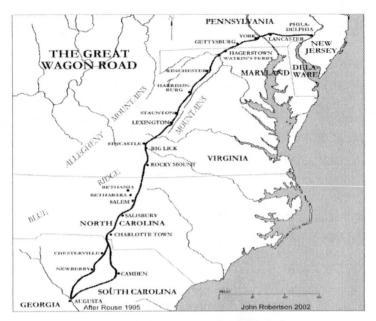

Map of the Great Wagon Road
prepared by John Robertson for
Come to the Cow Pens! by Christine R. Swager

were modest and not large enough to divide as the family grew so, as the children matured, they moved on south to establish their own homes.

Many settled in the area of North Carolina which became caught up in the Regulator movement. The Royal Governor, Lord Tryon, had taxed the people heavily for his palace at New Bern. The settlers in the back country paid taxes but had no protection from the Indians or outlaws, and they protested to the governor. When their complaints were met with indifference, they took action and were prepared to fight. The governor assembled his British troops and marched against the Regulators and defeated them at the Battle of Alamance on 16 May 1771. The victorious troops treated the prisoners harshly and hanged several.

Shortly after the incident there was a movement of settlers away from the Alamance region, many fearful of retribution from the vengeful royal governor. Some moved into the Indian country in western North Carolina which is now part of eastern Tennessee. Others moved south into South Carolina.

Although the largest group of Scots-Irish came in the early 1700's, several thousand came in subsequent years. Not only was the religious climate in Ireland hostile to these Presbyterians, but famine put additional pressure on the farmers to emigrate.

By 1730, South Carolina was encouraging Protestant settlers into the back country to provide a buffer against Indians attacks. Lutherans from Germany had already settled the area along the Santee and Edisto Rivers in the middle of the state. By 1750, the Scots-Irish were settling in western South Carolina.

After 1753, when Georgia became a British colony, settlers moved into that area. Earlier a few of the Scots-Irish had settled along the Broad River in Georgia which was Indian country. Then, after 1773, when the Ceded Lands were open to settlers, families who had settled in western Virginia, North and South Carolina, made their way into the new territory. Georgia had traditionally welcomed Protestants and the Presbyterians moved into the Wilkes County area. By the middle 1770's Scots-Irish settlers occupied territory from Georgia to Pennsylvania along the mountains. The mountains were the boundary of the Indian territory the British had promised to protect from intrusion.

The situation was perilous for the settlers but they were not completely isolated. They were connected by family, friendship and faith to all those other intrepid pioneers who occupied the back country. That relationship would be crucial as they faced the dangers in the wilderness and the conflict which was to come.

The new settlers brought to the back country the fierce independent spirit and determination which had developed over centuries. They now had land of their own and they intended to keep it. At first they built rude shelters as they cleared the land. The sod huts of Ireland were not practical in the mountains of the Carolinas and Georgia so timber was fashioned for log cabins. When sufficient building supplies were ready the neighbors came to help with the raisin' of a simple cabin of one or two rooms, with a dirt floor and a fireplace for heating and cooking. Some cabins were surrounded with a rough stockade to provide shelter for the settler and his neighbors in case of Indian attack.

Initially, the Indians had tolerated traders in their land as the traders were only there temporarily: these new settlers intended to stay. These Scots-Irish settlers adjacent to the Indian lands would be challenged again and again but they had established homes in the new land and they were prepared to defend them. In doing so, they would make their mark on Georgia history.

War Comes to Georgia—Chapter 3

The first concern of the settlers in the Ceded Lands was the security of their families. They expected Indian attacks and they were not long in coming. War parties of Indians, who were unhappy with the influx of settlers into what they perceived as their land, attacked and massacred families in the Ceded Lands. Unlike the royal governors of North and South Carolina who ignored the plight of their upcountry settlers, Georgia's royal governor, James Wright, used his considerable influence with the Indians to stop the bloodshed. However, before it was over, back country militiamen under the command of Elijah Clarke had retaliated on Indian villages. The behavior of both Indians and settlers was brutal. Elijah Clarke would figure prominently in Georgia's later conflicts.

Although the New Englanders had already challenged the authority of King George III, the Georgians in the back country were not immediately caught up with the fever for independence. This was partly because Georgia was a young and distant colony, and had little reason to complain of the British government actions.

In 1774, when coastal residents opposed British policies, back country militia leaders signed a petition supporting the British rule. They argued that they had no quarrel with England and perceived that to be Boston's problem. John Dooly and Elijah Clarke, who would later figure prominently at Kettle Creek, were among those who signed the petition. Their support for Governor Wright was not made on ideological grounds but was motivated by concern for the safety of their families. They depended on the King's troops to keep the peace in the back country. If those troops were withdrawn either for political reasons, or for strategic considerations such as moving the troops to quell the revolt in New England, the settlers would be more vulnerable to Indian attacks.

Although the settlers in the Ceded Lands were not eager to get involved, many settlers along the coast were agitating for independence, challenging Governor Wright's authority to govern. Those opposed to the British monarchy were called **Whigs**, or **Patriots**. Those who chose to support the King were called **Tories** or **Loyalists**. The settlers in the Ceded Land could no longer ignore the revolutionary fervor which had taken hold of Georgia.

In November of 1775, the Continental Congress authorized Georgia to raise troops. Since Georgia was sparsely populated, men were recruited from the Carolinas and Virginia. Although Georgia now had an army and a navy of sorts, problems arose since there was no agreement on who was in command. Politicians maneuvered to gain power for themselves as Georgia became more and more vulnerable.

On the night of 2 March 1776, British troops landed on Hutchinson's Island opposite Savannah and boarded rice barges. Local Whigs, determined to prevent the British from acquiring the rice, sent fire ships against the barges and burned some. The British sailed away with the rest of the rice which was sent to Boston to feed British troops there. Governor Wright, who had been under house arrest, saw the futility of his position and, eluding his guard, boarded a British ship and left the colony. This battle, known as The Battle of the Rice Barges, ended British rule in Georgia for a time. (O'Kelley, 2004, Vol. I:87).

However, it was not politics but self-preservation which motivated settlers to finally embrace the Whig or Patriot cause. Indian agents, who were officials of the British government, incited the Indians to attack the settlers. There had been Indian massacres in the back country from Georgia to Pennsylvania, targeting the Patriots and passing over the

Georgia Continental Officer
Arthur Edgar, Historic Site Manager
Fort Morris Historic Site

homes of Tories, or those loyal to the King. Now, it was clear to the Georgia settlers that the British were using Indians to intimidate those who opposed British occupation. Letters carried by a captured British officer confirmed the intentions of the British government to accelerate the Indian involvement. (McCall, 1909:296). The settlers reasoned that the British, allied with the Indians, were now the enemies of the people.

During the summer of 1776, Captain James McCall, a man the Indians supposedly trusted, was sent on a peace mission to the Indians. Captain McCall would later distinguish himself at Kettle Creek. However, in this instance, he was taken and held as prisoner until he managed to escape, but not without considerable torture. (O'Kelley 2004, Vol. I: 113). Another militia leader who would become important at Kettle Creek, Andrew Pickens, was campaigning against the Indians in western South Carolina. Life in the back country was becoming more and more perilous. (O'Kelley 2004, Vol. I:161).

By the summer of 1776, the Whigs were firmly in control of Georgia's government and Tory commanders in the militia were replaced by Whigs. Property of those loyal to the King was confiscated and, in order to force allegiance to the new movement of independence, many Tories were hunted down and humiliated. One method, tarring and feathering, not only held the victim up to ridicule but also inflicted considerable pain and injury.

The brutal treatment of a Loyalist, Thomas Brown, resulted in his feet being burned, (Cashin, 1999:28), and his acquiring the name of "Burn-Foot" Brown. This period saw many Tories leave Georgia for East Florida which had a strong British garrison. In East Florida, Tories would be organized into provincial units such as the King's Rangers under the command of Loyalist Lt. Col. Thomas (Burn Foot) Brown and the South Carolina Royalists. Brown would become a dangerous enemy of the Patriot militia as time passed.

England had sent units of the British Army to North America. These units are referred to as **British Regulars.** However, there were not enough of these well-trained and disciplined troops to deal with the vast expanse of territory which was America. Needing more troops, the British organized units of Americans who were full-time soldiers, equipped, uniformed, armed, trained and paid by the British. These units are referred to as **Provincials**, or **British Provincials.**

Some Provincial units had British–born officers such as Lt. Col. Banastre Tarleton of the British Legion, a unit recruited in the north, and Lord Rawdon of the Volunteers of Ireland, recruited from Irish neighborhoods around Philadelphia. Major Patrick Ferguson was another British officer who commanded Provincial troops in the south. Some Provincial units had American officers such as Lt. Col. John Cruger of DeLancy's Brigade of New York.

With increasing numbers of Loyalist refugees in East Florida, supplying them with food became a problem for the British. They looked to Georgia where food and cattle were abundant so raids into Georgia's territory were frequent. In an effort to neutralize East Florida as a British stronghold, Georgia planned attacks on St. Augustine three subsequent years but none were successful.

The first attempt to take St. Augustine was in August of 1776 and the expedition did manage to reduce settlements along the St. Johns River but failed to reach St. Augustine.

The following year another expedition was planned but those in command made no attempt to coordinate their efforts and that attempt failed.

The final attempt in 1778 had sufficient numbers of troops to accomplish the mission with Georgia Continentals, Georgia militia, South Carolina troops and naval ships but the operation broke down when commanders failed to agree on the strategy. Supplies for the troops were sparse and the weather conditions were miserable. Horses needed for carrying troops and supplies died on the march.

On 29 June 1778, British troops attacked Patriot forces at Alligator Creek killing thirteen and wounding several. With the weather deteriorating, forces scattered and supplies lacking, this expedition was abandoned. Now, as before, British raids on South Georgia resumed. (O'Kelley, 2004, Vol. I:199).

Meanwhile, the British had suffered reverses in the war in the north. After the Americans defeated General Burgoyne's British army at Saratoga in 1777, the French entered the war in support of the Americans. Now, unable to confront and defeat George Washington's army in the north, the British looked for another strategy. This would become known as the Southern Strategy. The intent was simple. The British would land troops in the south, take Georgia and the Carolinas. From there they would march to Virginia and cut off supplies to Washington's army.

The expectation of success in the south was predicated on the belief that large numbers of the settlers were loyal to King George III and only waiting for British troops to arrive. This British Army in the south would fight the battles, then move on while their local loyal subjects held the territory and maintained the peace. (Buchanan, 1997:26). It was a bold assumption which would later prove to be false.

In November of 1778, a coordinated invasion of Georgia was underway. British troops moved up from Florida, raided farms in Midway, took cattle and burned the buildings. At the same time a British force approached and occupied the port at Sunbury and demanded the surrender of the fort. This was the response:

We, sir, are fighting the battle of America...
as to surrendering the fort, receive this
laconic reply-- Come and Take It!

John McIntosh
Lt. Col., Continental Troop

Captain of Continental Artillery
Reenactor Sam Harrison, Continental Army Artillery

Lacking the force the take the fort, the British evacuated Sunbury. That fort at Sunbury was renamed Fort Morris in honor of an American officer who commanded the artillery at that encounter.

In December 1778 the British Army, under the command of Lt. Col. Archibald Campbell, arrived en force aboard fifty ships, landed just below Savannah and on the 29 December captured the city. (O'Kelley, 2004, Vol. I:216). In early January the British returned to the fort at Sunbury with sufficient force to take Fort Morris and, this time, the fort was surrendered after a brief bombardment.

Continental Artillery Unit

Fort Morris, a Georgia State Historic Site, is situated on the Medway River, at 2559 Fort Morris Road, Midway, GA.
It is located 7 miles from Exit 72 on I-95.

See: www.georgiastateparks.org/info/ftmorris

Lt. Col. Campbell lost no time in extending his control. With Savannah secure, and Sunbury reduced, he moved up the Savannah River toward Augusta. Campbell's troops took Ebenezer on 2 January 1779. On 14 January, the British offered full pardon to all Georgians who would take an oath of allegiance to King George III.

After Campbell occupied Augusta on 31 January, about 1400 Georgians took the oath of allegiance and were formed into Tory militia units. However, not all the settlers were eager to submit. Those who had taken an oath to support the British represented only about one tenth of the Georgians. There was especially strong resistance from the inhabitants in Wilkes County. Lt. Col. Campbell, determined to restore Georgia as a royal colony, initiated a campaign to subjugate the entire area. This effort would lead to the Battle of Kettle Creek in less than a month.

Patriot Forces in Georgia—Chapter 4

As the British commander, Lt. Col. Campbell, made plans to subdue the back country of Georgia, there were Patriot leaders who would challenge the British occupation of their territory. Since these men would figure prominently at Kettle Creek, as well as subsequently in the Revolutionary War, it is appropriate to introduce them here. Two, John Dooly and Elijah Clarke, were settlers in Wilkes County, while the others were neighbors living across the Savannah River in the Long Cane area (Abbeyville) of South Carolina.

Illustration by Dwight Ellisor.

John Dooly

John Dooly (sometimes spelled Dooley) was born into a Scots-Irish frontier family. (Davis, 2006:30-32). His father, Patrick, appears in the records of Frederick County Virginia as early as 1755, but moved to South Carolina backcountry about 1765. This son, John, the eldest of the family, inherited his father's possessions about 1768. By 1771 John was employed by the colony of South Carolina as a surveyor and was also a merchant. When the Ceded Lands became available he saw the opportunities available in the new land and claimed 700 acres on Fishing Creek and built a cabin. His two brothers also claimed land in the new area.

When disaffected Indians began a campaign of terror in the new lands, John Dooly was appointed colonel of the new militia. The concern of the settlers in the new territory was the Indian threat. In 1777, Thomas Dooly, John's brother, was captured, tortured and killed by Creek warriors. John retaliated against the Creeks by seizing a Creek peace delegation but was forced to release them. He had his revenge later when he led his neighbors against the Creeks in 1778. John Dooly was appointed as representative for Wilkes County in the state legislature and became that county's first sheriff. Although he had been preoccupied with providing safety for the region from Indian attacks, it would now be the British threat that faced Dooly.

When the British took Savannah and then moved to Augusta, all of Georgia was occupied except Wilkes County. Dooly, colonel of the Wilkes County Militia, appealed to Andrew Pickens, a resident of Long Cane and colonel of the Ninety-Six militia, for help. Pickens arrived in Georgia with two hundred (200) men to help the settlers resist the British incursion. Pickens, with more rank and experience than Dooly, would command the Patriot force at Kettle Creek.

Elijah Clarke

Elijah Clarke (later the family would drop the –e to Clark) was born in North Carolina in 1733. The Clarke family had been part of the Scots-Irish migration and had moved down from Virginia in the previous generation.

General Elijah Clark
(1733-1799)
Courtesy of the Augusta Museum of History

Elijah lived in the area of North Carolina which had been caught up in the Regulator movement. After the Battle of Alamance on 16 May 1771, the governor's troops treated the prisoners harshly and several were hanged. It is not certain to what extent Elijah Clarke was involved in the Regulator movement but he had many friends who were involved and some of those who were hanged were known to him.

Shortly after the incident there was a large movement of settlers away from the Alamance region, many fearful of retribution from the vengeful royal governor. Some moved into the Indian country in western North Carolina which is now part of eastern Tennessee. Others, like Clarke, moved into South Carolina. Whether or not Clarke moved to escape is not known, but for whatever reason, he settled at Grindal Shoals on the Pacolet River in South Carolina (near today's Spartanburg). He is believed to be the first white settler in this area. (Hope, 2003:47). The ground was swampy and not very productive, but game was plentiful and Elijah made a living hunting, trapping and trading in furs. He moved about the area and was referred to by early historians as the Daniel Boone of South Carolina. He was living in north-western South Carolina when he heard about the Ceded Lands in Georgia and made the decision to move again.

The new settlers moving towards the Ceded Lands carried their household belongings on carts and pack horses. They carried all the equipment they would need for life in this newly opened area. They carried seeds which would be required for planting in the land they would clear of timber. Cattle, sheep, hogs, and geese were herded along the trail. It would be a life of hardship and danger but many saw it as an opportunity.

Elijah Clarke, with his wife, Hannah, and their children settled on a creek in Wilkes County which they called Clarke's Creek. Elijah built a cabin with a stockade, or log fence, around it. It would be called Clarke's Fort. A fort at that time was merely a farm fortified against Indian attack. Family and neighbors could take refuge when danger threatened. Although the Indian chiefs had ceded the land, the new settlers realized that many young, hostile Indians would resist the settlers. The white traders and a few hunters who had traveled widely in the Indian country had posed little threat to the Indians. However, these settlers who were arriving in large numbers intended to stay. This alarmed the Indians and Clarke knew it was necessary to be prepared for attacks. They were not long in coming.

At Christmas, the Indians attacked settlers in Wilkes County and killed and scalped their victims. Elijah Clarke and his neighbors moved to repel the attacks. They realized that their safety depended on the settlers themselves. They organized and pursued the Indians meting out their own form of retribution. However, realizing they were outnumbered by the Indians and vulnerable to more attacks, they appealed to the royal governor for help. Governor Wright used the threat of military action against the Indians to force a sort of peace. However, it was an uneasy peace.

In 1778, when Georgia's government created a state army, Clarke was appointed lieutenant colonel. When the unsuccessful attack on British East Florida occurred in 1778, Clarke was wounded in the thigh at Alligator Creek. When the state troops were disbanded, Clarke became a lieutenant colonel in the Wilkes County militia which was commanded by his neighbor and friend, Colonel John Dooly.

By early 1779, Lt. Col. Campbell's British troops occupied Augusta, and detachments of the British army traveled the interior enlisting Loyalists into their ranks to put down the rebellion which we know as the American Revolution. Lt. Col. Elijah Clarke of the Wilkes County Militia was in the field, determined, daring, and ready to defend his home against the British, their Loyalist friends and their Indian allies.

In addition to Col. John Dooly and Lt. Col. Elijah Clarke, who were now living in Wilkes County, Georgia, there would be two more heroes of the Battle of Kettle Creek. They were Col. Andrew Pickens and Capt. James McCall, who were living in South Carolina, just across the Savannah River from Wilkes County. They were closely connected to the settlers in Georgia and shared the same Scots-Irish heritage.

Andrew Pickens

The Pickens family had migrated from Ireland and first settled in Bucks County, Pennsylvania, where Andrew was born on 19 September 1739. A series of Indian attacks in the area motivated the family to seek safer territory and they moved down the Great Wagon Road stopping for a time in Virginia. When Andrew was in his early teens, the family settled at the Waxhaws on the border between North and South Carolina (east of Charlotte).

During the Cherokee War Andrew fought with the British troops as a junior officer. After the war was over, Andrew Pickens moved to the Long Cane (Abbeville District). There he married and started a family. He raised cattle and traded with the Indians.

When war broke out between England and the colonists, Captain Andrew Pickens was involved in the first major battle in the south on 18-21 November 1775. South Carolina troops and the Whig militia attacked and took the powder which had been captured by the local Tories at Ninety-Six. A large Loyalist force sieged the American position. After three days the engagement was called off and the two armies dispersed. Captain James McCall was also involved in that battle and is listed as commanding a force of about fifty (50) Georgia militia, although the exact identity of that force is unknown. (O'Kelley, 2004, Vol. I:59-60).

On 1 August 1776, now promoted to major in the Ninety-Six District militia, Pickens participated in a campaign against the Indians at Seneca. (O'Kelley, 2004, Vol.I: 157-158). Again a large force of Georgia militia (240) participated in the bitter encounter.

Later on 10 August 1776, Pickens led a column of militia and scattered a party of Cherokees at Tugaloo River in South Carolina. The next day Pickens's troops, numbering about twenty-five, were surprised and surrounded by a force of about one hundred eighty-five (185) Cherokees. Forming his men in two rings he ordered them to fire in relays. Indians who rushed the ring were killed by hatchet, bayonet or knife. Pickens's men maintained their ring and their discipline until help arrived. According to historian Patrick O'Kelley, the Cherokee were awed by Pickens's heroism and this is when, regarding him as a great warrior, they named him Skyagunsta or Wizard Owl. The following day, 12 August 1776, Pickens' scouts engaged Cherokees at Tamassy.

The following month, at the Black Hole of the Coweecho River in North Carolina, Pickens was again involved in a campaign against the Cherokees. The American force included Lt. Col. Thomas Sumter's 6th Regiment of Continentals from South Carolina as well as Catawba Indians who were allied with the Patriots against the Cherokees who fought for the British. Among the Loyalist prisoners taken were 13 white men disguised as Indians. These men were referred to as 'white savages', and the Loyalists would continue this practice in Georgia throughout the conflict.

Now, in February of 1779, Col. Andrew Pickens met with John Dooly and assumed command of the combined Georgia and South Carolina militia which would fight in the upcoming conflict. Andrew Pickens had the experience in fighting both Indians and Loyalists, and was well known by the settlers in the back country.

Andrew Pickens was a devote Presbyterian. As an elder in the church he would become known as the Fighting Elder. He was reported to have been a dour Scot who rarely spoke and never smiled. He was, nonetheless, widely known and well respected by his neighbors. With his home close to the Savannah River, his neighbors included those Scots-Irish who had moved across the river into the Ceded Lands in Georgia. The command given to him by Dooly would not be a mistake. He would prove it at Kettle Creek.

General Andrew Pickens
(1739-1817)

Courtesy of Caroliniana Library

James McCall

Not only will James McCall become an important player in the coming Revolutionary War, he would campaign throughout that war in the company of Georgians. His son, Hugh McCall, would later settle in Savannah, Georgia, and write **The History of Georgia** in 1811.

The McCall family was part of the Scots-Irish migration and settled first on Conachcocheque Creek in Pennsylvania about 1730, where James was born 11 August 1741. To escape Indian attacks the family moved first to Virginia, and then to North Carolina.

In 1771, James McCall with his wife and three children settled on Little River, a branch of Long Cane Creek in the Abbeville District. Not only were they neighbors of Andrew Pickens but it is interesting to note the parallels in the two families' migration. It is known that often families and friends moved together as they migrated from settlement to settlement. It is very likely that the McCall and Pickens families were part of that pattern. Like Andrew Pickens, James McCall was active in protecting the western borders against Indian attacks.

At Ninety-Six, 19 November 1775, Captain James McCall is listed as commanding Georgia militia. Although the exact composition of his command is disputed, he was involved in the engagement.

In June 1776, McCall led a party of twenty men to conference with several Indian leaders. McCall's party was attacked and McCall was briefly held prisoner but escaped. The next month the Cherokee asked for a peace conference and indicated that they would deal with James McCall whom they trusted. Again the party was attacked close to Seneca and this time McCall and his men were taken prisoner. McCall was forced to watch the torture and death of many of his men. He was able to eventually escape by riding an unsaddled horse north to Virginia, rather than attempt to return home through the Cherokee nation. After joining

Virginia troops, he eventually made his way back to South Carolina.

In February 1779 he was serving in the South Carolina militia under the command of his neighbor, Col. Andrew Pickens and, in this company, he would fight at Kettle Creek.

In addition to the men mentioned here, there were experienced Indian fighters among the Georgia and South Carolina militia. Many were already acquainted through family, faith and friendship. They shared a common history of hardship and migration. This new land held great promise and they would fight to keep it.

The clothing of reenactor Fitzpatrick James Rhett Williamson, Elijah Clarke Wilkes County Militia, is probably typical of what the Georgia militia wore.

Loyalists Invade the Backcountry—Chapter 5

In early January, before he advanced on Augusta, Lt. Col. Archibald Campbell had sent a force under the command of Lt. Col. Boyd into the back country of Georgia and South Carolina to recruit, he hoped, thousands of Loyalists. There is little known about Boyd before he arrived on the scene in Georgia. Even his first name is in doubt. A later confrontation with Andrew Pickens suggests he was known to the locals. Robert Scott Davis, arguably the most knowledgeable scholar on the events of this area, reports that Boyd had been described by the British as a man who had lived in the frontiers of South Carolina. He may have been a resident of the area who traveled to New York and ingratiated himself with the British. If that is so, he was certainly successful considering the rank bestowed on him. Now a lieutenant colonel in the British forces, he would lead an expeditionary force into the back country.

Lt. Col. Campbell, still believing that the settlers in the back country would flock to the support of the King, envisioned a force of six thousand (6,000) Loyalists. With such a force, he would secure Georgia and attack the remaining rebels (Patriots) in South Carolina.

In addition to putting Boyd in the field recruiting in western South Carolina, he sent another of his officers, Major John Hamilton, into Wilkes County to recruit there.

Anticipating that he would soon have the force to attack South Carolina, Campbell sent a third officer, Major Daniel McGirth, up the Savannah River with orders to build boats for Campbell's troops to use to cross the river. Then they could attack General Williamson's South Carolinians who were camped on the other side.

Now the Patriots were confronted with four British forces in the back country of Georgia and South Carolina:

Lt. Col. Campbell and his thirteen hundred (1300) British soldiers in Augusta;

Lt. Col. Boyd recruiting in north-western South Carolina;

Major John Hamilton recruiting in Wilkes County;

Major Daniel McGirth building on the Savannah River.

Meanwhile, the Patriot forces were not idle.

General Williamson, who commanded 300 Continental soldiers and 1000 militia, was encamped across the Savannah River planning to prevent Lt. Col. Campbell's British troops from crossing into South Carolina.

General Ashe, with a force of twelve hundred (1200) North Carolina militia, was moving south across South Carolina to join Williamson.

Col. John Dooly and **Lt. Col. Elijah Clarke** were in Georgia trying to protect their territory and their neighbors from the harsh recruiting tactics of the British, especially Hamilton.

Dooly and Clarke appealed to General Williamson of the South Carolina militia to help resist the British in the back country of Georgia in general and to help deal with Hamilton in particular. Hamilton's methods were coercive and brutal. He recruited with threats of violence, claiming that those who refused to support the King were rebels and deserved hanging.

In response to the appeal from the Georgians, Col. Andrew Pickens and his militia from the Ninety-Six district moved across the Savannah River into Georgia and started tracking Hamilton. Capt. James McCall, who will often accompany Georgia forces, was riding with Pickens's force.

Hamilton, aware that he was being followed, moved to Carr's Fort and secured his position there. Col. Andrew Pickens, realizing that there was no source of water in the fort, began a siege knowing that thirst would eventually force Hamilton to surrender. However, Pickens's force was upslope of the fort, and they prepared a wagon with flammable material in it and planned to set it on fire and roll it down the slope into the fort.

Preparing a Fire Wagon
Reenactor John Thornton, Royal North Carolina Regt.

Learning that there were women and children in the fort, Pickens abandoned that idea and planned to let thirst force the Loyalists to surrender. As the siege continued, Pickens received word from his brother that Lt. Col. Boyd was moving toward Ninety-Six and forcing settlers to join his Loyalist force as he advanced. Since Pickens and the men riding with him were from the area around Ninety-Six, they were concerned for the safety of their families and neighbors. Col. Pickens and his militia hurriedly left Carr's Fort and rode towards Ninety-Six, leaving a detachment under the command of Capt. Robert Anderson to move north and prevent Boyd from returning to Georgia.

Major Hamilton, taking advantage of Pickens's absence, abandoned the fort and rode to the safety of Augusta and Lt. Col. Campbell's British troops.

Hamilton arrived in Augusta. Lt. Col. Campbell, realizing that there was no word on Lt. Col. Boyd's location, sent Hamilton back into north Georgia to find Boyd. Campbell also sent word to McGirth to stop building boats and to move into the back country to search for Boyd. Certainly the British forces were not getting information from the settlers in the area. Major Hamilton moved towards Wrightsboro and Major McGirth moved towards Carr's Fort.

Meanwhile, Col. Andrew Pickens and his Patriot militia had crossed the Savannah River into South Carolina to protect their homes in the Ninety-Six area. They soon learned that Boyd and his Loyalists were not moving in the direction of Ninety-Six, but were moving west to cross the Savannah River into Georgia. The fact that Pickens had information about Boyd's movements while the British did not, suggests that the settlers of the back country were willing to share their information with the Patriots, but not with the British.

Capt. Robert Anderson of the Ninety-Six militia with his detachment occupied McGowen's Blockhouse, which protected the approach to the crossing on the Savannah. It was the closest crossing to Augusta where troops could ford the river and, without boats, Lt. Col. Boyd would have to ford the Savannah River to get back to Georgia. With two swivel guns, Capt. Anderson was able to thwart Boyd's approach to the crossing there. Boyd moved his troops upstream looking for another place to ford. Capt. Anderson, now joined by other Patriot militia, moved across the Savannah to Georgia and tracked the Loyalists as they moved north on the South Carolina side.

When Boyd attempted to cross the river again using rafts and swimming the horses, Capt. Anderson and his militia attacked the Loyalists. Although the superior numbers of the Loyalists finally forced Anderson to withdraw, Lt. Col. Boyd reported 100 of his men, killed, wounded or missing. Many of the missing probably took the opportunity to return home.

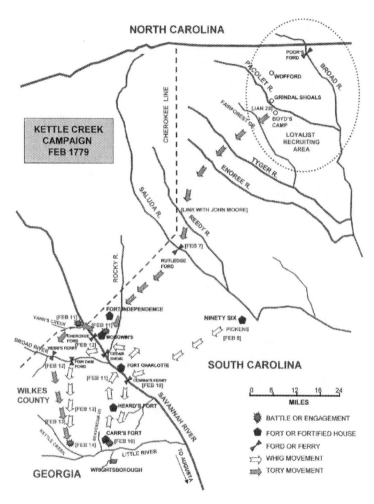

Map by Steven Rauch.

Movement of Patriot and British forces in the days prior to the Battle of Kettle Creek.

Although the British commander at Augusta did not know where Lt. Col. Boyd was, Col. Andrew Pickens knew exactly where the Loyalist troops were. Pickens and his men, now knowing that Boyd posed no threat to their homes, crossed the Savannah River into Georgia and were rejoined by Capt. Anderson and his detachment. Now Pickens's scouts had Boyd's men under surveillance and the Patriots followed a safe distance behind, not wanting their presence known until the opportune time to attack.

As Lt. Col. Boyd prepared to camp on the night of 13 February, Lt. Col. Campbell in Augusta still had no idea of where Boyd might be. However, Campbell expected that Boyd would have 6000 new recruits with him, giving the British a large enough force to attack the Patriot camp on the other side of the Savannah across from Augusta. When a loud disturbance with gun fire issued from Gen. Williamson's camp, Campbell believed that Gen. Ashe with 1200 North Carolina militia had arrived. Additional campfires in the Patriot camp convinced Campbell that the Patriot combined force now outnumbered his own. Lt. Col. Campbell withdrew his troops from Augusta at 2 AM 14 February and headed for Savannah. This left Campbell's three subordinate officers, Lt. Col. Boyd, Major Hamilton and Major McGirth, without the support of trained British troops in the back country of Georgia.

On 13 February 1779, a few hours before Campbell withdrew from Augusta, Lt. Col. Boyd and his newly recruited Loyalists set up a cold camp, (a camp without fires), in an area not far from present-day Washington, Georgia, which was then part of Wilkes County. The weather had been miserable and the troops were tired, wet and hungry. Boyd believed he was safe from attack and would reach Wrightsboro the following day. There, among settlers loyal to the King, he and his men would find support and comfort. Lt. Col. Boyd had no idea that Col. Pickens and his combined Georgia and South Carolina militia camped a few miles away.

The Battle of Kettle Creek—Chapter 6

When Lt. Col. Boyd and his Loyalists resumed their march on the morning of 14 February 1779, the men were tired, cold and hungry. In addition to the usual rain and cold, a strong wind increased their discomfort. Arriving at a farm in the area, the troops commandeered, or stole, the cattle which were pastured there. Moving on, they left behind a furious farm wife whose husband was riding with Lt. Col. Elijah Clarke's Wilkes County Militia which accompanied Pickens. When Pickens's Patriots arrived at the same farm, the angry wife was able to give considerable information about Boyd's troops and their route.

In the mid morning, Lt. Col. Boyd halted his troops along a fast moving and flooded stream, called Kettle Creek. There the Loyalist could build fires, slaughter the stolen cattle, and have the first hot meal they had had in days. The vegetation along the creek provided forage for their horses. The area where the troops camped was a flat area between the creek and a steep hill. Boyd, still unaware of Pickens and his Georgia and South Carolina militia, did station a few pickets on the hill. However, with the wind and rain, it is possible that the pickets did not expose themselves to the elements but hunkered down below the crest of the hill.

Boyd also sent a subordinate officer, Major William Spurgen, with a small detachment to look for a way for the troops to cross the swollen creek.

Colonel Pickens knew from his scouts the exact locations of Boyd's men and had time to meet with his subordinates and plan an attack.

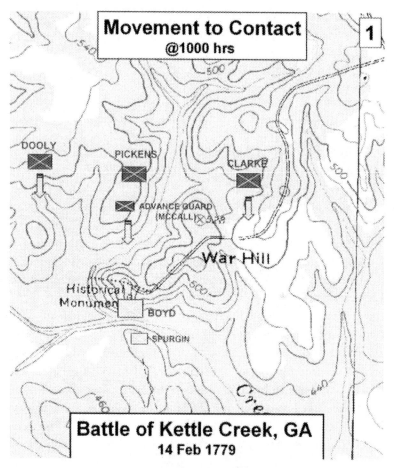

Map by Steven Rauch

It was decided that Pickens's force of about 200, most probably under the command of Capt. James McCall, would attack the hill. Col. Dooly with a force of about 100 Wilkes County militia would attack on the right and Lt. Col. Elijah Clarke with about 60 men would attack on the left. The total number Pickens had at his disposal was about 360. Boyd, on the other hand, commanded about 700, a force almost twice the size of the Patriot force. However,

Boyd's men had been recruited in northern South Carolina, while many of Pickens's force were local Georgians, or men who lived just across the river from their Wilkes County neighbors.

They knew the territory and they were fighting to protect their homes. There was loyalty among these locals and Pickens could depend on them to stay the course.

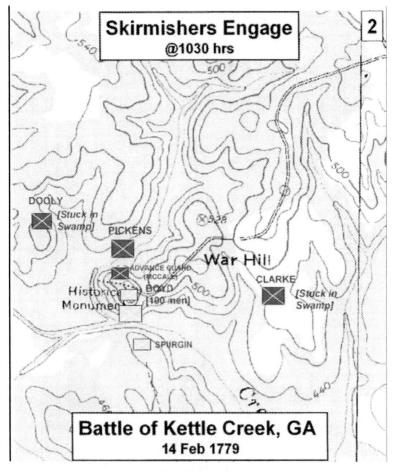

Map by Steven Rauch

Pickens ordered his men to advance but not to fire until he gave the order. However, Boyd's pickets on the hill spotted the Patriots and started firing, alerting the camp below. Boyd, with about 100 of his men, climbed the steep hill to see what was happening, and to establish a defensive line. Col. Dooly's troops were not in place since they had encountered rough going in the swampy area to the right. Some of the Ninety-Six Militia had moved to the right to flank Boyd and the Loyalists at the top of the hill.

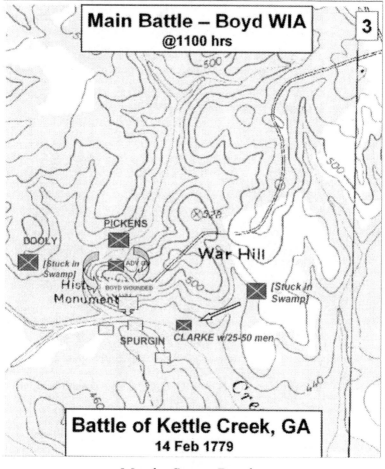

Map by Steven Rauch.
Note: WIA means Wounded in Action.

Seeing Boyd in his brightly colored British uniform, the Patriot militia fired. They were accustomed to aiming at the officers and, with or without a command to fire, they targeted Boyd. Three shots tore into Boyd and he fell, mortally wounded. The others fled down the hill in panic and the camp below was in chaos. Unable to get to their horses, many waded across the flooded creek.

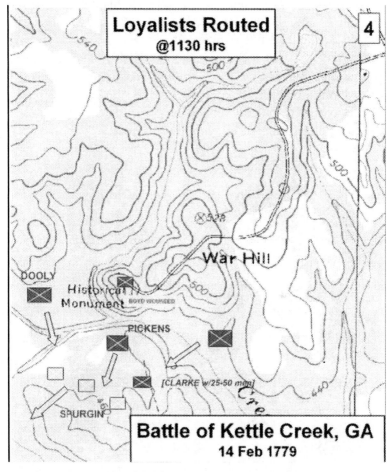

Map by Steven Rauch

Major Spurgen had managed to get across the creek with his men before the firing began. He now tried to assemble the fleeing Loyalists and regroup to meet the attack. Lt. Col. Clarke, seeing Spurgen's attempt to mount a defense, abandoned his orders to attack the left of the camp and charged across the creek. His horse was shot under him but he mounted another and, leading about two dozen of his men, rushed the Loyalists.

Meanwhile, Dooly had managed to get his men out of the swamp, joined Pickens and his men and overwhelmed the Loyalists who had not managed to escape across the creek. Dooly and Pickens then pursued the fleeing enemy. Major Spurgen, seeing that all was lost, led those who had escaped toward Wrightsboro.

It is reported that Pickens returned to the hill to pay his respects to the dying Boyd who, tradition has it:

Illustration by Dwight Ellisor.

He would proudly proclaim to all who would hear that he died for his King and country, while telling the pious Presbyterian Pickens that he wanted no prayers from a 'damned rebel' but that he would have succeeded if only he had not been shot. The victorious South Carolinian accepted personal items from the dying man to bring to Boyd's wife, a relation of Pickens. (Davis, **Kettle Creek,** 2006:34)

Pickens's Patriot force had suffered 9 killed, 21 wounded and 2 missing. Boyd's casualties were 70 killed or wounded, 150 captured. Although Major Spurgen attempted to lead the remaining Loyalists to Campbell's forces, only 270 reported to the British. The remainder of Boyd's force of approximately 700 probably took the opportunity to return to their homes.

Although Pickens had excellent intelligence concerning the back country, he was not aware that Lt. Col. Campbell had withdrawn his troops from Augusta. However, Pickens was under no obligation to pursue Boyd's Loyalist force. He had been charged with protecting the Georgia back country from the brutal recruiting of the British officers and that had been accomplished. The Patriot militia buried the dead on the field. Then, with the spoils of war, 700 horses, equipment and baggage which the Loyalists had abandoned, the Patriots disbursed; Pickens and McCall and their men back to South Carolina and Dooly and Clarke to their homes in Wilkes County.

Many of the prisoners taken at Kettle Creek were pardoned as it was felt they had joined the British under duress. However, several were charged with treason and five were hanged at Ninety-Six.

Although the Battle of Kettle Creek was a small engagement, it had considerable significance. It demonstrated that the British Southern Strategy had a serious flaw. Lt. Col. Campbell had embraced the British belief basic to the Southern Strategy, that great numbers of settlers were loyal to the King and would join the British when that army appeared in the south. The overwhelming support expected in Georgia and the Carolinas did not materialize as evidenced here. Campbell expected his recruitment would garner 6000 men. Boyd, the most successful of the lot, had managed to enlist only about 700. Although there were some who would pledge their support to the King, the majority of the settlers in Wilkes County were not among them.

What happened to the heroes of Kettle Creek? Many of those who fought at Kettle Creek would continue the struggle in Georgia, South Carolina and North Carolina. Their contributions to the cause of liberty are numerous and, to a large extent, unknown. We shall follow the Georgians in their continuing struggle.

After Kettle Creek—Chapter 7

Encouraged by the success at Kettle Creek, Major General Benjamin Lincoln, commander of the Continental Army in the South, looked to further success in Georgia. The emboldened Patriot militia mustered in increasing numbers giving the Americans cause to be optimistic.

Major General John Ashe of North Carolina led a combined force into Georgia determined to attack the British at the town of Savannah. General Ashe led his troops from South Carolina across the Savannah River and moved south toward Savannah with a force of about two thousand men.

Lt. Col. John Mark Prevost, an experienced officer, had replaced Lt. Col. Archibald Campbell. Although he was not familiar with the area along the Savannah River, he had been thoroughly briefed by Lt. Col. Campbell, who had held Augusta for a short time, and knew the area well.

On 3 March 1779, as the American Army camped at the confluence of Brier's Creek and the Savannah River, Prevost attacked. The battle was brief and disastrous for the Americans who lost as many as two hundred (200) killed, fifty (50) wounded and one hundred-seventy (170) captured. Many of the Patriots fled, some into the river where they drowned. The prisoners were marched to Savannah and were herded onto prison ships where many would die of neglect and abuse. (O'Kelley, 2004, Vol. 1:253-254).

At the time of the battle, Col. Dooly and his Wilkes County Militia were moving rapidly toward Brier's Creek intending to join Ashe's army for what they thought would be an attack on Savannah. They arrived at the scene of the battle too late to participate but were confronted with the task of burying the dead.

With the success at Brier's Creek, the British appointed Lt. Col. Prevost as lieutenant governor of Georgia in an attempt to restore colonial government. The royal governor, Governor Wright, who had fled the state during the Battle of the Rice Barges, returned. Now Georgia would once again be a royal colony. It would be the only colony England would be able to return to that status although the British intended to recover South Carolina shortly.

Although Savannah and the coastal area were firmly in British control, the back country was another story. There, beyond the reach of British soldiers, many settlers in the Ceded Lands were determined to continue their opposition. They were aligned with the Patriot militia in the back country of South Carolina, many of whom had been at Kettle Creek.

The Battle of Brier's Creek had convinced the Patriots that the British were too strong to be forced from Savannah. However, the British were vulnerable when they moved away from those fortifications. On 21 March 1779, Georgia militia commanded by Lt. Col. John Twiggs attacked about two hundred Loyalist troops at Beech Island, about 30 miles below Augusta on the Savannah River. The Loyalists were commanded by Major John Spurgin. Twenty Loyalists, (20) including Major Spurgin, were killed. The Americans suffered only three wounded. (O'Kelley, 2004, Vol. 1:266).

British commander, General Augustine Prevost, was poised to make a thrust into South Carolina and incited the Creeks to attack in that area. He warned the Loyalists there to wear red crosses and pine twigs on their hats so the Creeks could distinguish between Whig and Tory. The plan was thwarted when South Carolina militia under the command of Colonel LeRoy Hammond, crossed over into Georgia and attacked Loyalists and Creeks at Rocky Comfort Creek and killed ten and captured six. Only one patriot officer was killed in the encounter. (O'Kelley, 2004 Vol. 1:266).

Undeterred, Prevost marched on Charleston, South Carolina and planned an attack. Brigadier General William Moultrie was commanding the South Carolina Regiments and other Continental troops in defense of Charleston. The civilian authority in Charleston wanted to surrender the city and remain neutral rather than have the city attacked. General Moultrie announced he would not surrender but would resist. (O'Kelley, Vol. 1:277).

The British, in the area for three days, suddenly withdrew as they were short of ammunition. Also, Lincoln's army was approaching and the British commander did not want to be attacked from two sides by the Americans. The British retreat finally ended at Savannah, but not before several confrontations with Americans in coastal South Carolina.

In the back country, the conflicts continued. In July Georgia Colonel Benjamin Few attacked a war party in Wilkes County and drove the Indians off after inflicting serious damage. On 21 July, Georgia militia attacked a patrol of British soldiers who were escorting American prisoners to Savannah to be hanged. The British guards who survived the attack surrendered and the prisoners were released. (O'Kelley, 2004 Vol. 1:304).

While the Wilkes County Militia was patrolling the Ceded Lands protecting their homes from Indians, other Georgia militia under the command of Col. John Twiggs attacked a Loyalist force under the command of Lt. Col. Daniel McGirth. Twiggs drove off the Loyalist and captured prisoners, horses and arms. Part of Twigg's force captured drovers and the cattle they were driving to Savannah.

Although the area close to Savannah was firmly under British control, and Georgia was considered a royal colony, there was little safety for British and Loyalist troops who ventured far from that base. Still, the Americans did not have the strength to drive the British out of Savannah. However, that situation would change.

In late September 1779, a combined force of American and French forces arrived in Georgia south of Savannah. They were supported by the French Navy. Major General

Benjamin Lincoln was in command. Included in his command were troops of the First and Second Brigade of the South Carolina Continental Army, Georgia Continental troops, North Carolina Continental soldiers, Continental cavalry and artillery and militia from South Carolina and Georgia. The Georgia militia units were the Upper Richmond Militia under Colonel Benjamin Few, the Wilkes County Militia commanded by Col. John Dooly of Kettle Creek fame, and Colonel John Twiggs with his Burke County Militia. General Lincoln's American force numbered almost three thousand. (O'Kelley 2004 Vol. 1:314).

The French contingent, in addition to three dozen ships of the French Navy, included infantry of French soldiers, many of whom were Haitians. The number of French engaged was about forty-five hundred.

While the French and American forces lingered on the outskirts of Savannah for days contemplating a siege, the British commander, Major General Augustine Prevost, called in all of his men who had been detached beyond Savannah, and set about strengthening the fortifications of the city. One of the officers of the 2nd South Carolina Regiment of the Continental Line, Lt. Col. Francis Marion, who would later gain fame as a militia leader known as the Swamp Fox, exploded with the words: *My God! Who ever heard of anything like this before? First allow an enemy to entrench and then fight him!"*

After days of bombardment the attack finally was ordered and it was a disastrous affair. Prevost had had the time to build an almost impregnable position. It was beyond the ability of the allied force of French and Americans to take the city. With hurricane season approaching, the French withdrew their navy, and the exhausted American troops, having lost 125 killed and over 300 wounded, retreated to Ebenezer and then to Charleston.

Georgian historian, Kenneth Coleman, (1978) argued that had the attack on Savannah begun as soon as the troops arrived, the city might have been taken. The delay allowed

Prevost to strengthen his position. Francis Marion had been correct.

Hugh McCall (1909) describes the grave situation of the settlers in the Ceded Lands after the failed attempt at Savannah. Militia leaders were hunted down, their homes destroyed and women and children turned out of their houses and forced to flee on foot. Twiggs, Clarke and Dooly were targets as emboldened Tories now ventured into the Ceded Lands to threaten the settlers. Many Patriots were warned to leave the state under penalty of death.

With Savannah firmly under their control, England reassessed their strategy. The war in the north was at a stalemate. The British had been forced to evacuate Boston and Philadelphia and were concentrated in New York. The last time the British had engaged George Washington's Continental Army in the field had been in July of 1778 at Monmouth Courthouse in New Jersey. With the success in Savannah, England now looked to concentrate operations in the south.

At the end of February 1780, Sir Henry Clinton and Lord Charles Cornwallis arrived in Savannah with 14,000 soldiers, sailors and marines. (Stokesbury, 1991:229). Their destination was Charleston.

The British Siege of Charleston lasted about six weeks and ended on 12 May 1780, when General Lincoln surrendered. It was the greatest loss of troops in the war. America would never have another such catastrophe until World War II at Corregador. The loss of over 3000 Continental troops was disastrous. Among those troops were Georgians who were in the Continental Army. The professional soldiers, the Continentals, were taken prisoner, and many were confined in prison ships in Charleston where, under deplorable conditions, many died. The militia, or citizen soldiers, were given parole and sent home. By the terms of the parole, they were to remain neutral and not take up arms against the British. (O'Kelley, 2004, Vol. 2:35).

Sir Henry Clinton set about securing the territory by establishing outposts which would serve as areas from which the British would organize their Loyalist citizens into militia units. The outposts were situated in Georgetown, Cheraw, Rocky Mount, Hanging Rock, Ninety-Six, and shortly, Augusta. That ring of defense was intended to secure the backcountry of Georgia and South Carolina.

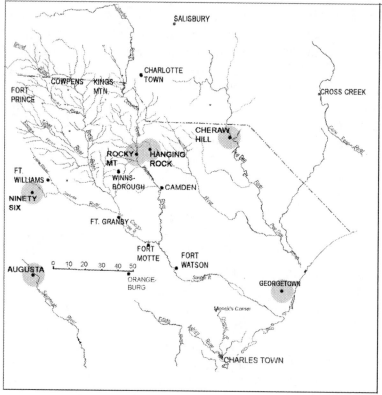

British Outposts in South Carolina and Georgia

(Prepared by John Robertson for **The Valiant Died** by Christine R. Swager)

Georgia Militia on the Move—Chapter 8

After the fall of Charleston and the establishment of outposts to control the back country, the British moved to consolidate their gains. Several prominent citizens were arrested and jailed. Some were shipped to the Islands as prisoners. Then the British called on the militia leaders to surrender their troops.

In South Carolina, General Williamson called on his officers to surrender and take paroles as he did himself. Most of his officers followed his lead including Colonel Andrew Pickens. However, one of the few officers who spurned the British offer of parole was Major James McCall who had fought at Kettle Creek and would, in the future, often fight in the company of Georgia militia.

In Georgia, the militia were also ordered to take parole and Colonel John Dooly did so. However, Lt. Col. Elijah Clarke denounced his former friends as cowards and traitors, and, with many of his Wilkes County Militia, took to the field in support of the Revolution. His anger against his former allies would fade as friendship overcame politics.

Militia units elected their own leaders and now, with former commanders on parole, new leaders emerged. In every case they were men who had fought against Indian attacks, and had fought British troops and their Loyalist militia. They were men who had shown courage in the face of the enemy and leadership qualities. In the Carolinas the new commander was Colonel Charles McDowell. In Georgia, the Wilkes County Militia appointed Colonel Elijah Clarke as their commander. It would not be long before these two commanders would join forces to oppose the British threat.

Although the focus of our story is the Wilkes County Militia of Colonels John Dooly and Elijah Clarke and the men they commanded at Kettle Creek, we would be remiss if we omitted the many other Georgia militiamen who now took the field.

In July 1780, Captain John Jones and thirty-five (35) Georgia militiamen of Burke County made their way across the mountains intending to join Carolina militia leader, Colonel Charles McDowell, on the Pacolet River north of the present city of Spartanburg, South Carolina. Aware that they traversed an area with strong support for the King, they pretended that they were Loyalists on their way to join the British at Ninety-Six. (Hope, 2003:40). Their presence would not go unnoticed for long.

On 12 July 1780, British Provincials under the command of Capt. James Dunlap attempted to surprise a camp of the Spartan Regiment at Cedar Springs (site of present day School for the Deaf and Blind in Spartanburg, South Carolina). Apprised of the British intentions, the Patriots had left fires burning and they hid in the wooded area around the springs. When Dunlap's men moved in to kill the men of the Spartan Regiment in their sleep, the British were met with gunfire and, silhouetted against the light of the campfires, had suffered several killed. The rest fled and some of the Provincials made their way to Gowen's Old Fort, a fort built to protect the settlers from Indians. It was situated on the present day boundary of Greenville and Spartanburg Counties.

As the Georgians moved across northwest South Carolina, they learned from local Loyalists of the soldiers in Gowen's Old Fort. They attacked and subdued the Provincials who had taken refuge there and forced them out. With no way to keep prisoners, the Georgians kept the weapons, ammunition and horses and paroled the Provincials and sent them marching toward Ninety-Six. This was 13 July 1780. Now Capt. Dunlap, who was in pursuit of the Spartan Regiment, was confronted with the Georgians who have taken Gowen's Old Fort. His attention now shifted to hunting down the Georgia militia. Dunlap will be an adversary of the Georgians from this time forward.

Late at night Jones and his Georgians arrived at Earle's Ford, and joined McDowell who was camped north of the Pacolet River. Tired from the long trip, they did not set up camp but stretched out to sleep at the edge of McDowell's camp. In the night, Dunlap approached the sleeping camp and, believing this was just a small company of Georgians, rushed the camp with sabers and bayonets. Jones's men were in the line of attack: two were killed and Jones received eight saber cuts on his head, but survived. (O'Kelley, 2004 Vol. 2:202). When the attackers intruded on McDowell's camp, there were more casualties, one a young boy.

When Dunlap realized that he had encountered a huge militia encampment, he made a hasty retreat down the road toward safety. The aroused camp mounted a patrol on fast horses to pursue the retreating Dunlap. The Patriots cut down Provincials as they overtook them, killing thirteen. (O'Kelley, 2004 Vol. 2:203). The Patriots stopped only when the Provincials had reached Fort Prince in modern day Spartanburg. Not knowing what personnel and armaments were in Fort Prince, the Patriots returned to Earle's Fort with thirty-five (35) horses and all the arms and equipment they could gather. As they returned past the dead Provincials they did not stop to bury them, but left the corpses to the ravages of scavengers and the weather. Reports of the events referred to the dead, unburied Provincials, as 'carcasses.' The war had lost all pretence of civility.

Now, the British evacuated Fort Prince where a modern marker denotes the place in a Spartanburg neighborhood. In three days the British had been ambushed, pursued and defeated. The casualties suffered by the British and their Provincials were just the beginning of the carnage which would follow. The Georgians would contribute to it all, not just in their own state, but in North and South Carolina as well.

After the British had been driven out of Gowen's Old Fort and Fort Prince, the Patriots looked to the last British fortification in the back country, Fort Anderson, which had been built to protect the settlers during the Cherokee Wars. It was known locally as Fort Thicketty since it was near Thicketty Mountain.

Col. Elijah Clarke and his Wilkes County Militia met with Colonel McDowell's force at Cherokee Ford. The wounded John Jones turned command of his Georgians over to Clarke and they were integrated into Clarke's militia. Additional militia from beyond the mountains arrived commanded by Colonel Isaac Shelby.

Many of Shelby and Clarke's men could have been acquainted since, before the battle of Alamance, 16 May 1771, they had lived in that area of North Carolina. When conditions there became dangerous, Clarke had moved to South Carolina and then to Georgia. The Shelbys, accompanied by many families, moved across the mountains into Indian country which is now eastern Tennessee. Shelby's militia was known as the Overmountain Men and those who survived living in Indian country were a hardy and courageous group. The men who rode with Shelby and Clarke may not have been personally acquainted but they shared the same culture and history, and were deeply committed to protecting their homes and families.

On 30 July 1780, the combined force moved against Fort Thicketty and demanded its surrender. Although the Loyalists defending the fort were well armed, they surrendered without firing a shot. The Patriots were able to replenish their supply of ammunition as well as muskets from the surrendered fort.

The British officer responsible for the occupation of the back country was Major Patrick Ferguson. His subordinate was Captain James Dunlap who had already clashed with South Carolina and Georgia militia. Now, on 8 August 1780, Dunlap moved against Clarke's camp which was close to Cedar Springs (in present-day Spartanburg). Clarke broke camp and moved north to Wofford's Iron Works

Colonel Isaac Shelby
Commander of Overmountain Men
Reenactor Dennis Voelker
Company of Overmountain Men

as Dunlap's force pursued. A running battle ensued with Clarke and Shelby standing to fight, then retreating to find another spot to defend.

In the conflict, Elijah Clarke was wounded twice; a saber wound to his head and another to his neck. The blow to his neck was deflected by his sword belt which mounted militia wore slung around their neck and across their chest. Without the belt, the wound could easily have been fatal. For a brief period Clarke was grabbed by two of Dunlap's men, but seeing his teenaged son, Capt. John Clark (notice his son had dropped the 'e'), was in difficulty, Clarke threw off the men holding him and returned to the fight.

Captain Dunlap retreated and was met by Ferguson's force. The British resumed the chase. The battle raged along several miles until the Patriots reached the Pacolet River and maintained the high ground from which they could thwart any attempt by Ferguson and Dunlap to dislodge them. Although the reports of casualties vary, Clarke and Shelby lost only four men killed. The British lost possibly thirty men killed and Clarke held about fifty of the British force prisoners. (O'Kelley 2004 Vol. 2:233-235).

Flushed with success in their area, McDowell hoped for another successful thrust against the British and their Tory militia. Colonel Shelby's militia were reaching the end of their enlistment and were eager to return to their families, but were willing to strike one more blow against the enemy.

The Loyalists had established a post at Musgrove's Mill on the Enoree River. It was an ideal spot to grind their corn and wheat and to care for the wounds inflicted in the many skirmishes with the Patriots. The encampment was reported to consist of about two hundred (200) Tories.

The Patriot force under Shelby and Clarke left camp at sunset and circumvented the area where Major Ferguson and his British Provincials were camped about 4 miles to the east. Riding rapidly through the night they were joined by Colonel James Williams and men of his Little River Militia. This group was from what is now Laurens County and Union

Site of Musgrove's Mill
on the Enoree River

County, South Carolina. Since they lived in the area, they knew the terrain well. (Graves, 2002:31).

The Patriots hoped to surprise the encampment at Musgrove's Mill but were detected by a Tory patrol. In addition, the Patriot commanders learned that the Tory encampment had been reinforced during the night by British Provincial troops from Ninety-Six under the command of Lieutenant Colonel Alexander Innes. The Patriots were outnumbered so a direct frontal attack was not possible.

The Patriots hastily threw up breastworks along a ridge across the river from the British encampment and hoped for a British attack. Williams commanded the center of the line with Shelby on the right and Clarke to the left. (Graves, 2002:33). Also, mounted detachments were on the flanks, hidden from view of the British and Clarke had an additional force of about forty in reserve. To entice the British into the range of their fire, a Georgian of the Wilkes County Militia, Captain Shadrick Inman, took a small group of expert riflemen and rode forward to skirmish with the British.

As Inman's men attacked, then withdrew, they lured the British closer and closer to the Patriot line. Ordered not to fire until the enemy was within killing range, the Patriots held their fire until the British line was within 60 yards. The first volley shocked the British line but it recovered and attacked with bayonets. Finally, Shelby's men were driven off their breastworks by bayonet. Elijah Clarke, seeing Shelby in trouble, attacked with his reserves and pushed the British back.

Now, Shelby's militia recovered and, with a battle cry that chilled the British, resumed the battle. In a later war that would be known as a 'Rebel yell,' but it was an Indian war whoop that the mountain men adopted from the natives. From this time forward Shelby's Overmountain Men would be known to the British as 'the yelling boys.' Now, with Shelby's position recovered, the mounted reserves rode into the battle.

As the battle raged, the British commander, Lieutenant Colonel Innes received two severe wounds and the mounted Provincial commander was shot from his horse. Other British officers dropped from wounds or killing shots and the battle was over. Again, accounts of the enemy dead are varied but the consensus is that the British lost 63 killed, 90 wounded and 70 captured. The American loss was four dead and nine wounded. Sadly, one of the dead was Captain Shadrick Inman of Georgia's Wilkes County Militia. He was buried on the field. (O'Kelley, 2004 Vol. 2: 286-292; Graves, 2002:33).

Seeing the enemy was abandoning the Musgrove's Mill camp, the jubilant Patriots intended to follow them to Ninety-Six and attack the British post there. However, word was received that the Continental Army had suffered a disastrous defeat at Camden by British forces under the command of Lord Cornwallis. Also, Patriot militia leader General Thomas Sumter had been defeated at Fishing Creek.

Knowing that the British could now turn their total attention to securing their hold on South Carolina, the three Patriot commanders opted to return home. However, before they parted they made a decision that would dictate Patriot militia strategy in later battles. Seeing how effective their combined militia had been, Shelby, Clarke and Williams decided to keep in touch and, when one was threatened, they would all come to help. They would not allow the British commander in the back country, Major Patrick Ferguson, to overwhelm one area at a time. They would mass the Patriot militia to meet future threats. Later, that decision would dictate the response to the British threats at King's Mountain and Cowpens.

Attack on Augusta—Chapter 9

Elijah Clarke, now back in Georgia, was obsessed with Augusta. His long time enemy, Lt. Col. Thomas Brown with his King's Rangers, occupied the town and the feelings of hatred ran deep and in both directions. It had been in Augusta before the British occupied Georgia, that the Whigs had injured Thomas Brown with a blow to the head, tied him a tree and threatened to burn him. Then, Brown was tarred and feathered and paraded in a cart through a jeering crowd. (Cashin, 1999:28). The hot tar had burned Brown's foot badly, and he lost two toes. From that time he was called 'Burn Foot' Brown. Now, at Augusta, he was commanding a unit of Provincials, Americans who were trained, armed and paid by the British. In addition, Brown supplemented his unit by recruiting Indians. He was no friend to the locals!

Clarke had an additional reason for wanting to attack Augusta. The town was a trading place and the Indian traffic in the area was a problem. In addition to the trade goods stored there, gifts for the Indians were distributed from that site. The British government sent large quantities of gifts for the Indians to insure their friendship and allegiance to King George. That alliance between Indians and the British put pressure on the Wilkes County settlers as they were living with the British to their east and the Indians to the west. It was not a comfortable situation.

Clarke hoped to muster a force of a thousand men (Rauch, 2005:4) and sought the aid of his old friend and ally, Major James McCall. McCall had served under Andrew Pickens and urged his former commander to return to the fight. However, Pickens had taken a parole and argued that he had given his word and, unless the situation changed, he was bound to keep it. McCall, still committed to the Patriot cause, met Clarke with about eighty men, far fewer than either Clarke or McCall wished to take the field. Additional troops from South Carolina, under the command of Major Samuel Taylor, joined Clarke giving him a total force of not more than six hundred.

Clarke planned the attack sending McCall to the south, Major Taylor on the north. Clarke and his Wilkes County Militia would make a frontal attack on Augusta. The action started on 14 September 1780. (Rauch, 2005:6).

At first the plan worked very well. Major Taylor surprised the Creek encampment. While Brown rode to support the retreating Indians, Clarke had captured Fort Grierson and its cannons. Brown, now realized that he was in a perilous situation, and sent word to the British at Ninety-Six that he needed reinforcements. Meanwhile, he fortified a house at McKay's Trading Post and directed its defense even though he had been wounded by shots through both thighs.

The siege of Augusta lasted until 18 September when Lt. Col. John Cruger arrived with his Provincial troops from Ninety-Six. The frontiersmen had to retreat in such haste that they were forced to leave their wounded behind. Now, the Indians who had been with Brown pursued the fleeing Patriots with brutal results. One hundred of those who escaped the initial engagement were captured.

What happened after the siege was broken and Clarke's troops were forced to retreat is in dispute. However, Hugh McCall reports:

Captain Ashy and twelve of the wounded prisoners were hanged on the staircase of the White House, where Brown was lying wounded, so that he might have the satisfaction of seeing the victims of his vengeance expire. (1909: 486).

McCall also reported that others faced a more brutal end as they had been turned over to the Indians to be tortured and killed.

Brown, later addressing that accusation, insisted that he had always followed the rules of war. (Cashin 1999:120). Even if that were the case, it was Lord Cornwallis's orders to hang those who had once taken parole and then rejoined the Patriots. Lt. Col. Cruger carried out that order. He believed that all who were in rebellion against the King deserved hanging without a trial. Cruger pursued the Patriots for some distance and took prisoners. Those he felt were prominent citizens were held hostage in prisons where many of them perished.

Jesse Gordon, who had fought at Kettle Creek, reported in his pension statement that he was one of 21 hostages taken by Lt. Col. Cruger and imprisoned for five months before escaping. Retaken by Tories, he was conveyed in irons to Brown's fort in Augusta. (Gordon, 1833). On the other hand, McCall reported that Clarke paroled the British officers and soldiers he had taken prisoner.

There was some criticism of Clarke and McCall's attack on Augusta since it would lead to relentless persecution of the Patriots in the back country. However, without the arrival of Lt. Col. Cruger's troops from Ninety-Six, the attack might have succeeded. As it turned out, the defeat was costly. Tories who supported the British now were emboldened and attacked the Patriots in the region. In the relentless pursuit of the Patriots over one hundred dwellings in Wilkes County were plundered and burned. One of the victims was John Dooly.

When John Dooly and Andrew Pickens took paroles, the understanding was that they would cease their resistance to the King and remain neutral during the conflict. In return, the British would honor their neutrality. However, before Sir Henry Clinton returned to his base in New York, leaving Lord Cornwallis as commander of the Southern Strategy, he changed the rules. He now decreed that those with paroles must swear allegiance to King George III and take up arms in His Majesty's forces. That meant that these former Patriots must now fight against those friends and neighbors who still opposed the British.

Many felt that, since the rules had been changed, they were no longer honor bound to abide by the paroles. However, Andrew Pickens had given his word and he intended to keep his part of the bargain even if the British had not. The British made several offers to Pickens, trying to get him to support the British cause. He remained stubbornly neutral.

John Dooly, however, may have been having second thoughts about his parole. If so, he did not have the opportunity to change his mind. In the campaign of terror after the failed attack on Augusta, neighboring Tories broke into his home and, in front of his terrified wife and children, killed him. This certainly was a violation of the protection the British paroles had promised!

Although Elijah Clarke had been furious with both Pickens and Dooly for abandoning the cause, it was Elijah and his wife, Hannah, who came to bury Dooly and assist his widow and children. Dooly was buried on his property which is now part of Elijah Clark State Park in Lincoln County, Georgia. The approximate burial site is marked at Dooly Springs. Dooly County is named in honor of Colonel John Dooly.

There is another incident related to Dooly's murder. It is the legend of Nancy Hart. The group of Tories who killed Dooly moved on to the cabin of Benjamin and Nancy Hart. Nancy was described as ugly with red hair and crossed-eyes. There is little doubt but that she was a woman of tremendous physical prowess and courage who had fought off Indians in the attacks on her home.

When the Tories arrived at her cabin they killed her turkey and demanded that she cook a meal for them. As the Tories drank and recounted their deeds at Dooly's, Nancy started cooking but, when the Tories were distracted by rum, she removed each weapon she could and passed them out through the chinks in the cabin to her daughter, Sukey, who was about twelve years old according to accounts. She directed Sukey to call Benjamin and the men working in the nearby fields.

Marker at Elijah Clark State Park

Before Benjamin arrived the Tories realized what Nancy was doing, but she grabbed a musket and threatened to shoot the first one who moved. Since, the story goes, her eyes were crossed, the men didn't know which one she was aiming at so didn't try to disarm her.

When Benjamin arrived he was accompanied by John Dooly's brother, George, who now learned of his brother's murder. The men wanted to shoot the Tories but Nancy insisted they be hanged and she personally hanged two of the Tories in her yard. (Ellet 1900:263-269).

Hart County and its county seat, Hartwell, are named for Nancy Hart. This is the only county in Georgia named for a woman.

Elijah Clarke had no choice but to quit the area and move his friends and neighbors to safer territory. The last of September, when those who would follow him mustered, there were three hundred men accompanied by four hundred women and children. (McCall, 1909:490). There was no safe haven in Georgia or South Carolina, but the British had never been able to breach the mountains. In the valleys of what is now eastern Tennessee Clarke had friends. He had recently fought at Musgrove's Mill with Isaac Shelby and had campaigned against the Indians with John Sevier. Their settlements would be his destination. The area he sought for refuge was two hundred miles from Wilkes County and the fall weather was deteriorating. They had rations for five days and the trip would take longer.

It would be a dangerous trip but with the Indians to their west; Brown, Tories and Indians to the south; and Cruger to the east, they had no choice. Pursued by enemy forces, including a former neighbor, Thomas Waters, it was necessary to move rapidly. Waters commanded a group of Tories, Indians and 'white savages', men who were white but went to war against their neighbors painted and dressed as Indians. Clarke reported that the stragglers who were captured by Waters were turned over to the Indians to be tortured and killed. Draper supports this claim that thirteen of the prisoners from Augusta were turned over to the Cherokees and killed by tomahawk; others were hanged. (Draper, 1881:200).

When the British learned of the movement of the settlers of Wilkes County, they planned to intercept and capture Elijah Clarke. The officer commissioned to perform this task was Major Patrick Ferguson, a regular officer of the 71st Regiment of Foot, the Frazier's Highlanders. He had assembled a cadre of Provincial troops from Ninety-Six and recruited about nine hundred Tories. This force, trained and equipped at Ninety-Six, set out to find Clarke. Expecting that Clarke would take the roads through South Carolina, Ferguson moved to that area. Clarke, however, moved his company along the trails just east of the mountains. It was an arduous trip, but would avoid British troops which used the roads.

As Ferguson campaigned along the border between North and South Carolina, he had captured a cousin of Isaac Shelby and sent him with an ultimatum to Shelby. The gist of the message was to come and declare allegiance to the King or Ferguson and his troops would cross the mountains, hang the rebels and lay waste their settlements with fire and sword.

The men who lived beyond the mountains were men of great strength and courage, and were not easily intimidated. When Shelby got the message he was enraged and contacted his friend, Colonel John Sevier, who commanded North Carolina's Washington County Militia. They agreed that such an ultimatum was a challenge which could not be ignored. At Musgrove's Mill, the three commanders there, Shelby, Clarke and Williams, had agreed that the way to meet the British force was with massed militia. Shelby and Sevier decided that would be the response to Ferguson. They sent word to militia in Virginia and North Carolina to prepare to move. The initial meeting place was Sycamore Shoals (north of present day Elizabethton, Tennessee).

The militia who assembled at Sycamore Shoals were men who lived on the land as they traveled. They carried dried corn, maple sugar, and little else. They did not need a commissary or a large supply of provisions. They carried their rifles, tomahawks and scalping knives. Their meager food supply could be supplemented with game. They were a self-sufficient unit and were a fearsome group. Proud of the homes they had established in the mountains, they were prepared to protect them. However, they would not fight in their own territory. They would take the war to Ferguson.

As Elijah Clarke and the Georgians moved toward Mount Pisgah and Mount Mitchell, they despaired of crossing the mountains where the snow was three feet deep. (Hays, 1946:108). It was in this vicinity where they encountered other Patriot militia who were moving to join Shelby. At this point they learned of the threat Major Ferguson posed.

Clarke realized that Shelby's strategy was sound. Always a warrior, never one to turn his back on such a challenge, Clarke was constrained by his responsibility for the welfare of the people he led. They had been on the trail for days and were exhausted and hungry. Clarke could not shirk this responsibility to join Shelby. Nevertheless, he sent 30 of the Wilkes County Militia under the command of Major William Candler and Captain Stephen Johnson to join Shelby. It is widely believed that Elijah's son, John, was a member of the group although his name does not appear in the roster since documentary evidence is lacking. These Georgians would participate in one of the most important battles in the Southern Campaign. (See Appendix II). The men Clarke encountered knew the area and told the Georgians of a pass through the mountains which would take them to the Watauga settlement.

As Shelby moved south, he was joined by militia from western Virginia, and North Carolina. As he approached the border of South Carolina, Colonel James Williams, his co-commander at Musgrove's Mill, joined him with his Little River Militia. Draper (1881:227) reports that it was to Williams's command that the Georgians became attached. Again, these Georgians were acquainted with Col. Williams and his men from their assault on Musgrove's Mill.

As the combined militia rested at Cowpens on the night of 6 October, they learned that Ferguson was to the east and moving closer to Charlotte where Lord Cornwallis was camped. Determined to deal with Ferguson before that officer could get protection from the larger British force, a thousand of the assembled Patriot militia mounted their horses and moved toward the east on the morning of 7 October 1780. The men chosen were those who had the freshest and fastest horses, and they forded the Broad River and moved toward King's Mountain where they had learned Ferguson was encamped.

The afternoon of 7 October 1780, the Patriot militia from across the mountains in what is now eastern Tennessee, from western Virginia, from North and South Carolina, and from Georgia surrounded Ferguson's force at King's Mountain. One of the officers with the Loyalists later reported that when he heard Shelby's 'yelling boys' whom he had faced at Musgrove's Mill, he knew the battle would be fierce. It was. In the battle that followed, the Patriots killed Ferguson and one hundred and fifty-six of his force, wounded another one hundred and sixty-three, and took the remainder of the force, six hundred and ninety-eight prisoner. (O'Kelley, 2004 Vol. 2:322-340).

Of the Patriot militia involved, it is estimated that twenty-eight were killed, and sixty-four wounded. Colonel Williams of the Little River Militia was mortally wounded, and died shortly after the battle and was buried in the area. (Graves, 2006:52-54).

While his Georgians were fighting at King's Mountain, Clarke finally arrived in Watauga Valley with his refugees from Georgia. They had traversed two hundred miles in eleven days. The settlers in Watauga Valley greeted them warmly, fed them and found shelter for the entire group. McCall reports that the women and children remained there 'until the storm of the war was over.' There would be much more action for the Georgians before that time arrived.

After King's Mountain—Chapter 10

After Major Patrick Ferguson was killed at King's Mountain, and his force was killed, wounded or taken prisoner, the British had to rethink their strategy. Lord Cornwallis had moved as far north as Charlotte, North Carolina, in his march toward Virginia. Now, realizing that there were hundreds of Patriot militia on his exposed western flank, he moved his headquarters back into South Carolina at Winnsboro.

Lord Cornwallis may have thought that he would have a winter camp to recover his losses. In the north armies suspended hostilities and camped for the winter and Lord Cornwallis had experienced that when he served with the British there. However, the Patriot militia had no intention of allowing the British time to regroup. The victories over the British since Charleston had been militia victories and after King's Mountain, the number of militia in the field increased and they intended to maintain pressure on the enemy.

Until now, Lord Cornwallis had little to fear from the Southern Continental Army. The British had defeated that force at Camden and the shattered remains of that army had retreated to Hillsboro, North Carolina. However, as Lord Cornwallis traveled the treacherous winter road to Winnsboro, General Gates moved his Continental forces towards Charlotte. Now General George Washington would make a decision which would change the war in the south. He assigned a new commander to the Southern Army: Major General Nathanael Greene. Washington had great confidence in this general who has been described as having a superior mind and a Herculean memory. Events would prove that Washington's confidence was justified.

Charles, Lord Cornwallis
Reenactor Trent Carter, 33rd Regt. of Foot

Meanwhile, with the families from Wilkes County now safely residing in Watuaga Valley, Elijah Clarke assembled his militia and moved south. Militia General Thomas Sumter was campaigning in western South Carolina and Clarke joined Sumter. Other Georgians arrived, commanded by Colonel Benjamin Few. Soon the Georgians attached to Sumter's force numbered about 100. Among the troops were Major James McCall and his South Carolina State Dragoons.

While encamped at Fishdam Ford on 9 November 1780, Sumter's force was attacked by British forces at midnight. Sumter's had been rather cavalier about security and the attack came as a surprise. The Georgians, who had set up a separate camp with their own security, were able to repulse the British. After the shock of the surprise at Sumter's camp had dissipated, the Patriot forces fought off the attacking force and wounded and captured the British commander. (O'Kelley, 2004 Vol. 2:355-359).

Lord Cornwallis, feeling that Sumter was a threat that needed to be neutralized, sent Lt. Col. Banastre Tarleton to track down and annihilate Sumter's troops. Tarleton was the most capable of all of Cornwallis's officers but he was known to the Patriots as Bloody Tarleton as his dragoons had butchered American prisoners at Monck's Corner and at the Waxhaws. The most hated of all British officers in the South, he was a successful cavalry officer in whom Cornwallis had great confidence. With cavalry, infantry and artillery, Tarleton moved to find and destroy Sumter's force. Learning that Sumter had moved south of the Tyger River, Tarleton rushed to attack leaving his artillery and much of his infantry behind.

On 20 November 1780, Sumter, realizing that Tarleton was close at hand, positioned his troops at Blackstock's farm. He posted the Georgian riflemen behind the fence which bordered the road. When Tarleton's cavalry rode up the road, the Georgians shot several of the troopers out of their saddles and turned the British back. After Tarleton regrouped and sent in the infantry he had with him, the British found themselves in a cross-fire which inflicted more

Tarleton's Legionnaire
Reenactor Tony Scotti, British Legion

casualties and Tarleton pulled back to wait for his artillery and remaining infantry to catch up with him.

Knowing that his troops could not withstand an attack with artillery, Sumter planned to withdraw. Sumter, suffering a serious wound from scattered shot which penetrated his shoulder, turned the command of the field over to Georgia's Col. Twiggs. Now, with painful wounds and shrapnel lodged in his spine, a profusely bleeding Sumter was carried from the field and moved across the Tyger River. Col. Twiggs built campfires and appeared to be maintaining the field. However, he evacuated the camp in the darkness, crossed the Tyger River, and moved to safety. (O'Kelley 2004 Vol. 2:365-372).

The Battle at Blackstock's was clearly a Patriot victory. However, in his account, Tarleton (1787) claimed victory and listed the American casualties as considerable including three colonels killed. One of his own officers (McKenzie, 1787) refuted that and described the battle quite differently. He wrote that the enemy, the Patriots, were well protected by the fence and a log cabin and, with the exception of Sumter, there were few casualties. Although the number of casualties vary with accounts, even accounts of British officers on the field agree that the British lost many officers, dead and wounded. American accounts estimated the number of British killed at about one hundred.

The Georgians departed from Sumter's force and Elijah Clarke and Benjamin Few took their militia back to the Long Cane area (near Abbyville). They were accompanied by Major James McCall and his South Carolina Dragoons. McCall's home was in the area and, it can be supposed, the homes of many of his men were in that vicinity. Clarke's intention was to raise a sufficient militia force to attack the British post at Ninety-Six. Recent militia successes had encouraged recruitment. Also, the Continental Army was now based in Charlotte and troops under the command of Brigadier General Daniel Morgan were campaigning in the western Carolinas.

When the British commander at Ninety-Six learned of Clarke's intentions, he sent a force of about 250 soldiers to attack Clarke whose total force was about 100. On 12 December 1780, Clarke and his troops were caught between a Loyalist militia force and Provincial troops at Long Cane. Clarke and McCall battled their way out of the trap but 14 of their men were killed, 7 wounded and 9 captured. Two of the wounded were Elijah Clarke and James McCall. McCall's wounds were superficial and he would be back in the saddle within days. Elijah Clarke, however, was critically wounded and carried from the field. (O'Kelley 2004 Vol. 2: 381-383).

Many of the Provincial troops returned to Ninety-Six leaving Captain James Dunlap to continue to pursue the Patriots in the area. The British believed, at first, that they had killed Elijah Clarke. When it was learned that he was critically wounded but still lived, James Dunlap was determined to find him.

Dunlap's troops attacked the home of James McCall and, not finding either of the men they sought, they destroyed the property and terrorized the family. The troops plundered even the family's clothing leaving Mrs. McCall and her children destitute. This act of brutality would not be forgotten nor forgiven by Clarke and McCall.

Next Dunlap made a mistake which would have an impact on the rest of the war. He attacked the home of Andrew Pickens. Dunlap knew that, although Clarke and Pickens had disagreed about Pickens taking parole, they had been friends in the past and had campaigned together. Dunlap reasoned that, since Pickens's home was near the scene of the battle, Clarke might have found a safe haven there. Dunlap's troops destroyed property and terrorized the inhabitants of Pickens's home before they left, without finding Clarke.

Andrew Pickens was a man of honor. He had made a pledge and he had kept his word. The British had treated him somewhat differently than others on parole. Dooly, for example, had been murdered. However, knowing the respect Pickens commanded in the area, the British had hoped to persuade him to change his allegiance. They had offered him land, money and a commission in the British Army but Pickens had been resolute in his neutrality. Now, the British had violated his property and an irate Pickens announced that he had kept his word but the British had not kept theirs. He was now under no obligation to continue his parole and would return to the fight, knowing he would have a 'halter round his neck.' This term was applied to those who had returned to the fight after taking parole. If they were captured by the British, they would be hanged.

Andrew Pickens lost no time in returning to the field. The Continental Army under General Daniel Morgan was encamped at Grindal Shoals on the Pacolet River (near present day Spartanburg, SC). Morgan's army was called The Flying Army since it was intended to move rapidly. However, the force was much smaller than any that the British would be able to move against it. Morgan needed help.

On Christmas Day Andrew Pickens reported to Morgan at Grindal Shoals. He was accompanied by a small number of his old militia, including James McCall. Morgan gave Andrew Pickens the command of the militia which needed to be mustered to support the Continental Army. Realizing that Morgan needed a much larger force than accompanied him, Pickens left to summon the militia in the back country.

McCall remained with the Continentals and was attached to Lt. Col. William Washington's Virginia Cavalry. Learning of the approach of Lt. Col. Thomas Waters, the old enemy from Georgia, Lt. Col. Washington and McCall moved their mounted troops to intercept Waters. Waters had assembled a group of Loyalists from Georgia and was moving to join the British at their post at Ninety-Six. As he made his way across northern South Carolina, he was plundering and terrorizing the inhabitants.

On 30 December 1780, Washington and McCall found Waters and his Tories at Hammond's Store. Seeing the overwhelming force against them, the Tories (Loyalists) attempt to escape. Washington gave the order to the troops to attack with swords and they did. Cutting down the Tories as they tried to escape, the Americans killed or wounded one hundred fifty (150), and captured forty (40). (McGee, 2005). Waters managed to survive and escape. There was not one casualty among the American Patriots.

The year had started with the British expectation of controlling Georgia and South Carolina. Now, at the end of the year, it was obvious that their campaign was in trouble. The militia had inflicted serious casualties on the British forces. Now the Continental Army was in the area determined to do the same.

Daniel Morgan Moves South—Chapter 11

Lord Cornwallis was alarmed that Lt. Col. Washington had defeated Loyalist troops at Hammond's Store. He felt that his post at Ninety-Six was threatened.

Major General Nathanael Greene had ordered part of the Continental Army under the command of Brigadier General Daniel Morgan to western Carolina to annoy the enemy and spirit up the settlers. Greene moved his own headquarters to Hicks Creek on the PeeDee River at a spot close to where Cheraw, South Carolina is today.

Lord Cornwallis could see the problem. If he moved his full force against Morgan to the west, Greene could threaten the British post at Camden and, possibly, the port of Charleston. If Cornwallis moved against Greene to the east, Morgan would move against the British post at Ninety-Six. The British commander had no choice but to split his army. He ordered the British Legion, the 17th Light Dragoons, a battalion of the 71st Regiment of Foot and the 7th Regiment of Foot to be detached from his camp to pursue and destroy Morgan. To command this elite group he chose Lt. Col. Banastre Tarleton, his most effective cavalry officer. Although the Americans considered Tarleton a brutal officer, he was a favorite of Lord Cornwallis.

As Andrew Pickens sent out word in the upcountry for the militia to muster, surely every settler knew the consequences if Tarleton were to destroy Morgan's Continental force. A British victory seemed certain and no settler would be safe from the brutal Tarleton.

When General Daniel Morgan knew that Lt. Col. Tarleton was pursuing him, Morgan started moving his American

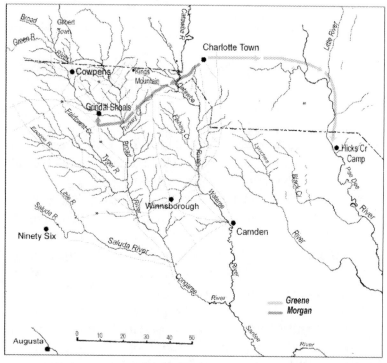

Greene divides and repositions his army

Map by John Robertson for **The Valiant Died**
by Christine R. Swager

troops to the northwest. This would lead Tarleton further and
further from Lord Cornwallis's headquarters at Winnsboro.
It would also give Morgan and Pickens more time to gather
militia. Morgan's small force was outnumbered two-to-one
in infantry and three-to-one in cavalry by Tarleton's force.
To make matters worse, Tarleton's command included
British regular and Provincial troops who were well trained,
disciplined and experienced.

A confrontation between the two armies would be
conventional. Each side was armed with muskets and that
weapon determined the tactics. Opposing infantries would

fire ordered volleys until one side weakened. Then a bayonet attack would end the conflict. Although this seems strange to us now, it was standard procedure at the time, and for good reason. The muskets had an effective but inaccurate range of about fifty yards. By firing a volley into the enemy line, the scattered shot would shock and intimidate as bullets tore into flesh. Each weapon had to be reloaded after every shot, so there was a pause between volleys, and experienced soldiers could load and fire about four times a minute. Cannons also had to be reloaded after every shot. Mounted soldiers with their sabers could strike down infantrymen or artillerymen if they could reach them while they were reloading.

The militia in the back country was composed primarily of riflemen and riflemen had rarely fared well against regular British troops in the field in a conventional battle. The rifle had a longer range and was much more accurate than the musket but was slower to reload; having no bayonets, the riflemen were vulnerable to bayonet and dragoon attacks.

Morgan was himself a rifleman and an Indian fighter. He boasted that a good rifleman could hit a man at three hundred yards, and hit him in the head at two hundred yards. Morgan also knew the fears and limitations of the militia but he needed them if he were to have a chance to survive an attack by Tarleton's troops.

When Morgan received reports that Tarleton was close behind and moving rapidly, the decision was made to do battle at Hannah's cow pens. The terrain was acceptable to Morgan and the area was well known to the militia. It had been the camp of the militia on 6 October 1780, the night before they attacked Ferguson at King's Mountain.

On 16 January 1781, Andrew Pickens and several militia units joined Morgan at what will become known as the Cowpens. Other militia units arrived all day and late into the night: four battalions of the Spartan Regiment, the Little River Militia, North Carolina Militia, Virginia Militia, and the Georgians.

The Georgia militia had been scattered into several small units as their campaigns had taken them far from their families and farms. Now they came together in three small companies commanded by Major John Cunningham with subordinates, Captains Joshua Inman, Richard Heard, and George Walton. They would fight at Cowpens under the command of Major James Jackson and Major John Cunningham.

Brigadier General Daniel Morgan
Reenactor Bert Puckett, Second South Carolina Line,
Continental Establishment.

With these reinforcements Morgan had a Flying Army of about six hundred (600) men complemented by a thousand (1000) militia. (Babits, 1993:55-56). How could those units be combined into a cohesive fighting unit and face one of the most ruthless and determined British commanders? It would have been impossible for anyone but a general such as Daniel Morgan.

Daniel Morgan was a different sort of general at a time when general officers were gentlemen: educated, affluent and powerful. Commissions were given to foreign officers who were, if not titled, at least very well connected. Daniel Morgan was poor, uneducated and without any of the attributes of a gentleman. However, he was, according to some historians, one of the finest battle field commanders this nation has ever produced. John Buchanan asserts: **"If one were to judge him by all who have led Americans into battle, he would have no superiors and few peers."** (Buchanan, 1997:276).

Daniel Morgan first appeared on the Great Wagon Road when he was a teenager. He was unaccompanied by family or friends so little is known about his early life. He never spoke about it. He worked as a wagon driver and, by the time he was twenty, he owned his own team. He delivered supplies in wilderness areas over faint, or non-existent, trails. He knew the backcountry. He settled in the Winchester, Virginia, area and was known as a brawler, drinker, womanizer, gambler - a man who would accept any challenge. He was considered the strongest, fastest and 'baddest' character in the area. However, when Indians threatened, Daniel Morgan could be depended upon to defend the inhabitants and punish the Indians.

In the French and Indians Wars (1753-1763) Morgan, with his team, was impressed by the British Army to accompany Braddock's Campaign. One of the officers with Col. Braddock was another Virginian, George Washington. Both were with Braddock's troops in July 1755 when Braddock was killed and the British defeated. The British officer was buried in the road and the wagons driven over the spot so the body could not be found and violated by the Indians. Morgan emptied his supply wagon and loaded it with wounded and drove them to safety. (Higginbotham, 1961:6).

However brave and dependable Morgan was to the British, it was at this period that an event occurred which would color Morgan's attitude for the rest of his life. Not a man to accept authority, he had defied a British officer and then struck him, rendering the officer unconscious. The punishment was 500 lashes with a cat-o'-nine tails. Although such a sentence would kill a lesser man, Morgan survived with the flesh on his back hanging in shreds and his boots full of blood. (Higginbotham, 1961:4-5). Morgan, thereafter, harbored a great hatred for British officers. Tarleton would be the epitome of what Morgan despised.

After the war with France was concluded, there were conflicts with Indians in the Ohio territory. Morgan commanded Virginians in a campaign against the Indians to protect their families in western Virginia. By the time of the American Revolution, Morgan was well known to Virginians. When another Virginian, George Washington, was appointed Commander of the Continental Army, he had the authority to enlist troops. When the Americans had British troops confined in Boston, Washington needed more troops. He authorized Daniel Morgan to recruit Virginian riflemen and move them to Boston. Morgan not only recruited the finest shots in his territory but he moved them to Boston, marching 600 miles in 22 days.

The citizens of Boston lived like typical Englishmen and had never seen men such as accompanied Morgan. They were dressed in the hunting frocks of the riflemen. Many, including Morgan, wore a breech-clout and high leather moccasins. In addition to the rifles, which were not typical of firearms in that area, they carried tomahawks and scalping knives. If the Bostonians thought to ridicule this group of backwoodsmen, that idea was soon dispelled when Morgan's men had shooting matches to relieve the boredom. Typically the target was the size of an orange placed on a branch at over 200 yards. Not only were the Bostonians impressed but the British soon found that it was not prudent to raise heads above the parapets. A head at 200 yards posed no difficulty to these sharpshooters. (Higginbotham, 1961:19).

Although these new troops had exceptional skills, they were unaccustomed to the boredom of camp life, and had no inclination to obey authority. When an expedition was organized by Col. Benedict Arnold, Morgan's men were chosen to accompany him. The intent was to move through

Maine and attack Quebec. The expedition started from what is now Augusta, Maine, in November. They moved up the Kennebec River and when bateaus, flat cargo boats, carrying their supplies had difficulty moving against the swift current, it was Morgan and his men who waded into the freezing water to push the boats. The account of that trip is an adventure that we have no time for here. However, when the Americans attacked Quebec, the mission failed. It was no fault of Morgan who led his men courageously. The attack was poorly organized and Morgan found himself isolated and surrounded. He was taken prisoner and spent the rest of the winter in the cold and dismal jail.

As was the custom of the time, prisoners were exchanged. When Morgan returned to America, he had to wait until a British officer of equal rank was exchanged. As soon as that occurred, Morgan was active again and commanded rangers accompanying Washington's troops.

In June 1777, a new threat appeared. The Northern Army of King George III was poised in Canada to attack. The commander was Major General John Burgoyne. The intent was to move down into Vermont and capture Lake Champlain. From there the British would move overland to the Hudson River and then march south and capture Albany, the capital of New York. Burgoyne expected that the British Army in New York City would move north along the Hudson and meet him at Albany. With the Hudson River under British control, General George Washington would be cut off from New England. The British believed that the contentious New Englanders were the source of the rebellion and if they were isolated, the rest of the country could be brought under British control. Of course this was more than two years before the British moved to the south!

The British expedition left Quebec with seven regiments of the British army, five German regiments, French-Canadian boatmen, and Indian scouts. The grand procession included wives and children of the officers with their servants. (Murray, 1998:1). It was reported that Burgoyne's personal baggage contained wagons of fine wine.

At first Burgoyne's campaign was successful and the fortifications on Lake Champlain fell to the British. However, the trek overland was a different story. The British soldiers had to cut through forest and swamp and build roads for the baggage and the camp followers. It was an inhospitable terrain and the troops were plagued by insects as well as local residents who attempted to impede their progress.

George Washington had sent an army under the command of Major General Horatio Gates to confront Burgoyne. Gates was accompanied by General Benedict Arnold who was still a loyal and competent American officer. While the two armies were still far apart, a situation arose that required Washington's attention. The Indians accompanying Burgoyne were terrorizing the settlers in the area. This situation was beyond the control of either Burgoyne or Gates. General Washington, however, knew of the solution to the Indian problem. He detached Colonel Daniel Morgan and his Virginians to join General Gates.

Although Burgoyne's British Army had suffered a defeat at the Battle of Bennington when New Hampshire militia took the field under Col. John Stark, (Murray, 1998:62), it was at Freeman's Farm near Saratoga on 17 September 1777 where Col. Daniel Morgan and his rangers inflicted severe damage on the British. Accompanied by American infantry to protect them from a charge by the British infantry with bayonets, Morgan's men stationed themselves along the tree line and even in the trees and obeyed the commands Morgan gave using a whistle made of a turkey bone.

The British charged repeatedly across the cleared area: Morgan's men shot them down. Burgoyne reported that the British artillery was useless as the riflemen shot the artillerymen as they served the guns. Observers reported twenty men killed or wounded at the sides of the cannons. (Higginbotham, 1961:68). When Burgoyne finally had to retreat from the field, his army had suffered almost 700 men killed or wounded. (Murray, 1998:75). Burgoyne would later report that he was defeated at Saratoga because of the casualties suffered at the hands of Daniel Morgan's rangers. However, Burgoyne's attempt to reach Albany was not over.

After a few days to rest and restore his shattered army, General Burgoyne attempted an attack on General Gates's American Army on 7 October 1777. During the fierce fighting, British General Simon Fraser rode among his soldiers, attempting to reorganize his troops when it appeared that all was lost. His conspicuous gallantry was not lost on the American troops. Morgan ordered one of his most capable riflemen to shoot Simon Fraser and it was done. According to the story, the rifleman was Tim Murphy and he made the shot from a tree at three hundred yards. Morgan had every confidence in his riflemen. (LaCrosse, 2002:137; Higginbotham, 1961:73).

After General Burgoyne's surrender of his army he met Daniel Morgan and complimented him on the finest regiment of rangers in the world. Burgoyne knew the value of Morgan but the Continental Congress did not. While others were advanced in rank, Morgan was not. The disgruntled Patriot resigned his commission and returned to his home in Virginia. He pleaded ill health and, considering the abuse his body had taken over the years, it was not surprising that he suffered from rheumatism and sciatica.

The defeat of the British at Saratoga was a turning point of the war in the north. It necessitated a change in British policy which led to the Southern Campaign. When General Gates, who had commanded at Saratoga, was sent to confront Lord Cornwallis in the south, he needed Daniel Morgan and prevailed upon Congress to recall him to active service. Now, with a commission as a brigadier general, Morgan traveled south but not soon enough to be involved in the disastrous Battle of Camden. General Gates had placed the North Carolina militia in the battle line confronting the most experienced of Lord Cornwallis's troops. When the British advanced with bayonets, the militia fled. Lt. Col. Banastre Tarleton had pursued the fleeing troops cutting them down as they ran.

Now Daniel Morgan, at the cow pens on the night of 16 January 1781, moved from campfire to campfire, greeting militia, telling stories, complimenting their successes and their abilities. He wore a hunting shirt and no emblems of his rank except a sword. He needed nothing else. These men knew of him. There had been few great American successes on the field other than Saratoga and Morgan's heroism was known to these men in the back country.

Morgan was one of them: poorly educated, rough, hard, and fearless. He talked of the victory of tomorrow and how the old folks would praise them and the young girls kiss them for their bravery. He might even have lifted his shirt to show the scarred back which has been described as rough as alligator hide. He had a score to settle with British officers and Benny, as he called Tarleton, would learn that in the morning. (Babits, 1998).

Morgan explained to the militia what he wanted them to do. Although they knew the risks they were taking, he promised that his infantry would protect them from the British bayonets and William Washington and James McCall's mounted would protect them from the sabers of Tarleton's horsemen. No commander had ever asked more of militia than Morgan did that night, but they trusted him. There was no officer in the American Army more worthy of the trust and respect of this militia.

The Battle of Cowpens—Chapter 12

Morgan had sent out scouts under the command of Georgian Capt. Joshua Inman to keep watch for Tarleton's approach. (Babits, 1998:58). They reported to Morgan before dawn on 17 January 1781 that the British were moving up the Green River Road toward Morgan's encampment. Morgan had not slept but prowled the camp throughout the night greeting late arriving militia. Now he awakened his rested troops with the news, "Benny is coming." The men ate food which had been cooked the previous night and moved to take their positions.

Major James Jackson of Georgia was appointed brigade major of Pickens's militia line, and the remainder of the Georgians, along with some South Carolinians, were assigned to fight under the command of Major John Cunningham. (Babits, 1998:38). They were posted on the left of the Green River Road as skirmishers. There were other Georgians who would ride with Major James McCall who commanded the mounted militia. Col. Joseph McDowell and the North Carolina militia were posted on the right side of the road as skirmishers. Those two units would be the first to encounter the British. Morgan had challenged the Georgians and North Carolinians as to who would be the better riflemen.

When Lt. Col. Tarleton and his British troops marched up the Green River Road to the edge of what would be the battleground, the British troops were already hungry and tired. They had been moving since 3:00 AM along poorly defined trails and in miserable weather. The night had been rainy with temperatures hovering around freezing. Some of the ground was partially frozen. Now about daybreak, the

97

Major James McCall
Commander of Mounted Militia
Reenactor Ron Crawley
3dCLD/McCall's Mounted State Troops

weather was bleak with limited visibility. However, Tarleton could see on the road ahead the Little River Militia prepared to challenge his progress.

Tarleton must have thought that this small force was to conduct a delaying action to allow Morgan's retreat with his Continental Army across the Broad River which was a few miles to the rear. Tarleton was determined to destroy Morgan and expected little resistance from this militia. He commanded some of his mounted to ride forward to survey the situation before he advanced with bayonets to clear the field. Certainly the militia would flee. Hadn't Tarleton been successful with these tactics before?

As the dragoons rode forward, they were surprised by the fire of the skirmishers who had been concealed among the trees on either side of the road well in advance of the militia. As the skirmishers fired, several British fell from their saddles and the remainder rode back to Tarleton. Now there was no time for Tarleton to waste. The skirmishers were within rifle range of the British line and several shots found their mark. Tarleton would have to retreat and regroup or deploy and press forward. He was not one to hesitate and the British line was forced to attack the militia with bayonets. British troopers were ordered in to scatter the skirmishers.

As the British started forward in battle line they were suddenly faced, not just with the Little River militia in the road, but a solid line of 1,000 militia, as the skirmishers moved back to the flanks, and other militia units moved forward. The British never wavered but moved at a quick pace, a slow trot, toward the militia. The British line was determined to sweep the field with their bayonets. (Babits, 1998:86).

Surprisingly, the militia line never wavered. In spite of the fact that they could have done considerable damage at three hundred yards, at two hundred yards, at a hundred yards, they held their fire. They had given Morgan their word to wait for the command to fire when the British were close and in killing range, and these were men who were determined to keep their word. The British were within fifty yards, still believing that the militia would bolt and flee, when the command was given for the Patriot militia line to fire. As directed, they aimed at officers and sergeants. As bullets found their marks, many in the British line fell to the ground.

The British quickly regained their composure and moved on, still determined to attack with bayonets. However, the militia left the field to regroup and the British were now faced with Morgan's Continental Army which had been waiting in full battle line. For most of the British, this was the first inkling that Morgan was still on the battlefield. Now the British, suffering many casualties already, faced a line of Continental soldiers who were ready and waiting. These Continentals were seasoned regulars who had fought many battles before and they were proficient in the use of the bayonet.

Now the confrontation reverted to conventional battle tactics. The two lines fired volley after volley. Finally Tarleton ordered in his reserves, the 71st Highlanders, with instructions to take no prisoners. The reserves attempted to flank the American line.

Then came what Babits refers to as a 'misunderstood order.' The Continental Infantry turned and moved away from the British line. It was not a retreat as the men trailed arms and reloaded their weapons as they marched. An astonished Morgan confronted the commander and selected a position on the field where the Continentals were to turn about and fire, then charge with the bayonet. The command was followed and the British, thinking they had the Americans on the run, and without their officers to retain order, were breaking ranks and pursuing the American line like a mob.

On command the American line turned and fired, most of them from the hip. The British were at point blank range. Then the American charged with the bayonets. The stunned British threw down their arms, fell face down on the ground in surrender, or started to run away from the battle.

Now, only the Highlanders continued to fight. William Washington and his mounted moved to the British right and

Andrew Pickens and the reformed militia attacked on the British left surrounding the Highlanders. The battle was over. Such a complete victory with the enemy surrounded is called a double envelopment. There are only three major battles in history which were concluded by a double envelopment. The Battle of Cowpens is the only such battle on this continent.

Tarleton attempted to save his guns, but that failed. He tried to get his mounted troops to assist the Highlanders but they refused. A defeated Tarleton left the battlefield with his mounted officers and staff, following his fleeing dragoons. In a battle which lasted about one-half hour he had lost one fourth of Cornwallis's troops, and all of the British light infantry. He left on the field his shattered army, over one hundred dead and more than two hundred wounded. One British officer, Lt. Roderick McKenzie, reported that at the end of the battle:

A number, not less that two-thirds of the British infantry officers, had already fallen, and nearly the same proportion of privates... (p. 178.)

The Americans would take over six hundred prisoners, capture over eight hundred muskets, two field pieces (cannons) and a portable forge.

Morgan reported that his losses were 12 killed and 60 wounded, but he was only counting those in his original Flying Army. Those numbers did not included militia casualties which Andrew Pickens reported as light. In Hugh McCall's History of Georgia he reports that three Georgians were killed and five wounded. However, the participation of the Georgians did not end at Cowpens.

General Daniel Morgan knew that Lord Cornwallis would march against him to try to release the British prisoners. Before noon Morgan had assembled the British prisoners and started their march toward the north. He left seventy-five of the British wounded on the field as they were too seriously

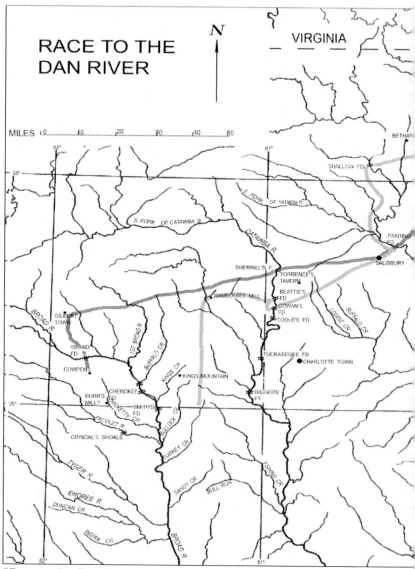

"Race to the Dan River" following Battle at the Cowpens. Darker gray shows approximate path of Morgan's/Greene's army. Lighter gray shows that of Cornwallis' army.

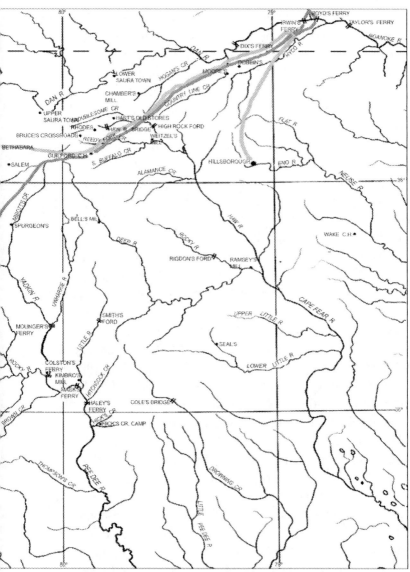

Map after Newberry Library and Malone, 1999.
Routes after "Another Such Victory", Baker, 1999.

Map prepared by John Robertson for
Come to the Cow Pens! by Christine R. Swager

injured to travel. The tasks of caring for the wounded and burying the dead were left to the local militia. Andrew Pickens took care of the wounded and secured the field, buried the dead and made arrangements for the wounded to be exchanged. When this had been accomplished, Pickens dismissed many of the militia units, but led his own militia which included James McCall, and the Georgia militia commanded by Majors Jackson and Cunningham, into North Carolina. For the next six weeks they would campaign in that state as they assisted the Continental Army in what is known as 'the race to the Dan.' (Buchanan, 1997:334-358).

There was no place to secure the prisoners in the south so, to move them out of reach of Lord Cornwallis, they would have to be moved across the Dan River, the boundary between North Carolina and Virginia. With Lord Cornwallis in pursuit it was necessary to move as swiftly as possible. Morgan sent the prisoners, guarded by Virginians, to the west, keeping his own army between the prisoners and the pursuing British.

Although Morgan had in his command mounted troops of Lt. Col. William Washington and Lt. Col. Henry (Light Horse Harry) Lee, most of his command was infantry and on the march. Morgan needed mounted to gather intelligence, find supplies, intimidate the local Tories and move anything which might benefit the pursuing British.

At Ramseur's Mill, Lord Cornwallis realized he was losing the race. The British Army traveled with a large supply train, carrying not only supplies for the soldiers, but the comforts that British officers took to the field: silver, fine china, wine, camp furniture and the like. The constant rain had made the primitive clay roads of North Carolina a quagmire, trapping horses and wagons in the mud. Lord Cornwallis made a decision which he surely will regret at a later time. He stopped and burned the baggage, keeping only a few wagons for wounded. He hoped to move more rapidly and overtake and destroy Morgan.

Major General Nathanael Greene, commander of the Continental Army in the south, joined Morgan at Salisbury and took command of the move towards Virginia. He lost the services of his finest officer when Daniel Morgan was forced to retire due to illness. The years of abuse Morgan's body had withstood resulted in rheumatism and sciatica so painful that he could not longer stay in the saddle and was carried to his home in Winchester, Virginia, on a litter.

Major General Nathanael Greene led his Continental Army across North Carolina toward the Dan River, pursued by a determined Lord Cornwallis. The 'race to the Dan' was won by Greene when he ferried his troops across the Dan River in the vicinity of present-day Danville, Virginia, on 14 February 1781. It had been a month of misery since the Battle of Cowpens: cold, rain and mud. Andrew Pickens and his militia did not cross the river with the Continental Army. They remained in North Carolina with orders to operate to the rear of the British advance and annoy the British to the greatest extent possible. (Buchanan 1997:362).

Within hours of the American crossing Lord Cornwallis arrived on the banks of the Dan River with his British Army. The river was too deep to ford, and all the boats had been moved to the north of the river where the American troops were now safe. Major General Greene was now in friendly territory where he could re-supply his army and feed the hungry troops.

On the other hand, Lord Cornwallis was in hostile territory without means of obtaining supplies and equipment to replace the baggage he had burned at Ramseur's Mill. The prisoners he had sought to rescue were now beyond his reach and would languish in prison at Fort Security close to York, PA, until they were released in the summer of 1783. Lord Cornwallis had also failed to destroy Greene's army and, in the chase across North Carolina, had lost 17% of his British Army to death, disease and desertion.

There was no advantage in being on the banks of the Dan River so Lord Cornwallis moved his troops south to Hillsboro, North Carolina, where he hoped to find friendly inhabitants who would help relive his suffering army. It was not to be. The area could not feed an army of that size. The account of a British soldier reports that such was the scarcity of food that they were "even obliged to kill some of their best draft horses." (Hagist, 2004:83).

Major General Greene was beyond Lord Cornwallis's reach, but he had no intention of remaining inactive. His ambition was to destroy the British Army and to accomplish that he had to leave the safety of Virginia and return to North Carolina. In preparation for his return he ordered Lt. Col. Henry (Light Horse Harry) Lee to move south, across the Dan River, and join forces with Andrew Pickens and his militia who were still trailing Lord Cornwallis's Army and gathering intelligence. On 21 February Lee returned to North Carolina to search for Pickens and his men. (Dunkerly, 2006).

After Lee joined forces with Pickens, they participated in what became known as Pyle's Hacking on 25 February 1781 at Haw River. Col. Pyle was escorting about 400 local Tories to support Lord Cornwallis when he encountered Lt. Col. Lee's Legion and Andrew Pickens's militia. Lee's Legion wore uniforms very much like those of the British Lt. Col. Tarleton's British Legion: short, green woolen jackets, leather helmets trimmed with bear fur. Pyle expected to be met by Tarleton and he mistook Lee's troops for Tarleton's. Lee realized the confusion and requested that he be allowed to pass. He later reported that he hoped to overtake Pyle and to dissuade the Tory leader from joining Lord Cornwallis. Lee led his troops past the Tories. Pickens and his militia were accompanying Lee. There is some discrepancy about how the ruse was discovered. Some reports suggest that the Tory militia recognized Pickens's militia as Patriot. Others suggest that one of Lee's officers, not knowing the pretence, attacked when he realized that the men he was passing were Tory. However, the American horsemen attacked with their swords and in a matter of minutes killed ninety-nine and wounded one hundred fifty of the Tories. The only American casualty was a wounded horse.

Lord Cornwallis considered the area close to his headquarters to be safe, and had ordered Tarleton to provide security for the Tory militia which he expected to join him. The attack at Haw River infuriated Cornwallis and it had serious consequences. It intimated the Tories, making it difficult for the British to gain support from the locals. Further, Lt. Col. Tarleton now attempted to find and annihilate Andrew Pickens but was unsuccessful.

At Wetzel's Mill on 6 March 1781, Lt. Col. Tarleton attacked Lt. Col. William Washington and Lt. Col. Henry Lee who were accompanied by Pickens's militia and Georgia militia. Although the British suffered more casualties than the Americans, Andrew Pickens was not pleased with the use of his militia and asked permission to return to South Carolina with them.

In fairness to Pickens, the hostilities in the back country of South Carolina had escalated after Cowpens with Tories and Indians emboldened by the retreat of Morgan from their area. Also, Pickens's militia had traveled hundreds of miles from their homes and been on the move for two months since the Battle of Cowpens. Some Georgians had left Wilkes County the last of September and made the exodus with their families to Watauga; some had fought at King's Mountain, Blackstock's, and Long Cane; and all had fought at Cowpens.

Major General Greene and Governor Rutledge agreed to the plan and released Pickens and his militia from the duty they had required of them. It would not be the last time that Greene would depend on Andrew Pickens and the Georgians, but for now, they were going home.

More Action in the Backcountry—Chapter 13

While the Georgians had been in North Carolina, Elijah Clarke had recovered from his near fatal wound and was ready to resume the campaign. He had a score to settle with Major James Dunlap and his British Provincials. Not only had Dunlap been a constant source of irritation, he had been at the battle where Clarke and McCall had been wounded and, in his search for them, had brutalized James McCall's wife and children and had violated Pickens's neutrality. Accompanied by Lt. Col. James McCall, who had returned from the 'race to the Dan,' Clarke went looking for Dunlap.

On 21 March 1781, Clarke and McCall, with a force of about 180 men, tracked Major Dunlap to Beattie's Mill in the Long Cane district. Dunlap was accompanied by local Loyalist militia but when they saw the size of the force against them, they fled. McCall secured a bridge to prevent Dunlap from retreating, and Clarke attacked. Dunlap ordered the remaining men to take cover in the mill. Clarke ordered his men to stay out of range of Dunlap's muskets, a distance of about fifty yards. Clarke's men with rifles could hit a target well beyond that range so they settled in and kept up a constant, well-aimed fire. Finally, with thirty-four of his men wounded or killed, a wounded Dunlap surrendered. (O'Kelley, 2005, Vol. 3: 162-164).

Previously, Pickens and Clarke had decided to send prisoners to Gilbert Town (now Rutherfordton, North Carolina), for internment until the officers could be exchanged for American officers of equal rank whom the British held prisoner. It was expected that Major Dunlap would be transferred to Gilbert Town but he never arrived.

There are differing accounts of what happened to Dunlap. Some accounts report that he died of his wounds and others that he was killed. It is widely believed the Georgians were responsible, executing what came to be known as 'Georgia parole.' Certainly Pickens believed that Dunlap was murdered as he offered a $1000 reward for the killer but no one collected it. Pickens considered the slaying a murder but surely those who had encountered Dunlap's brutality in the past considered it justified.

Major General Nathanael Greene and Andrew Pickens were attempting to conduct the campaign according to military conventions. Greene was especially distressed with the execution of prisoners. Although the Georgians may have been at fault in this instance, it would be a mistake to believe they were alone in this practice. Lt. Col. Tarleton's men had butchered prisoners at Monck's Corner and at the Waxhaws. Major James Wemyss and his regiment had burned out over fifty plantations in the Williamsburg District, hanged Patriots and burned Presbyterian churches, claiming they were 'workshops of sedition.' Lt. Col. Brown had hanged Wilkes County Militia prisoners at Augusta, and Lt. Col. Cruger, who commanded the British at Ninety-Six, ordered prisoners taken to be hanged without trials. There was brutality on all sides.

The success of the Georgia militia was short-lived. As they moved back toward the Savannah River and Georgia, many of the men came down with smallpox, a highly contagious and often fatal disease. Elijah Clarke was stricken and turned his command over to Lt. Col. Micajah Williamson, a veteran of the long campaign who had fought at Kettle Creek. Clarke then went into self-imposed isolation. Lt. Col. James McCall went to his home at Long Cane to wait out the illness but he died there. There is some disagreement as to whether he died in April or in May. However, this veteran of Kettle Creek and fourteen other engagements, lost his battle with smallpox and was buried in the vicinity of his home.

While Clarke was ill, his men went back to their Wilkes County properties for the first time since they had made the long trek to Watauga. They were appalled at the conditions: homes had been burned, crops taken, old men hanged and women and children turned over to the Indians as captives or to become victims of torture. The militia held Lt. Col. Thomas Brown, who commanded in Augusta, and Lt. Col. Thomas Waters, who commanded the Tory militia and Indians, responsible. There would be no peace in Georgia until those brutal officers were gone.

On 16 April 1781, Lt. Col. Williamson mustered Clarke's militia and joined Major Jackson and other Georgians in the vicinity of Augusta, hoping to siege the town and force Lt. Col. Brown from the area. However, the Patriot militia force was not strong enough to take the town. The middle of May a recovered Elijah Clarke arrived in the area near Augusta with one hundred additional troops and the situation would soon change.

While Clarke and his militia had struggled with smallpox, the commander of the Continental Army in the South, Major General Nathanael Greene, had altered the course of the war in the south. On 15 March 1781, just a few days after Andrew Pickens and the Georgians had left the Continental Army in North Carolina, Greene had engaged Lord Cornwallis's British Army at Guilford Courthouse, North Carolina. Although Greene had been forced to withdraw from the field, leaving the field and the victory to Cornwallis, the British Army had suffered a staggering loss of men and officers. (Baker, 1981:76). The British had been forced to march to Wilmington, North Carolina, to recover and re-supply.

General Greene had taken the opportunity to move his Continental Army into South Carolina with the intention of taking back all the territory the British claimed. By the middle of May, Greene had forced the British to evacuate Camden on the Wateree River, Fort Watson on the Santee River, Fort Motte on the Congaree River, Fort Granby on the Saluda River and forced the British out of their post at

Orangeburg on the Edisto River. Now General Greene and his Continentals were moving toward Ninety-Six, the last British stronghold outside of Charleston.

Andrew Pickens, promoted to militia brigadier general after his success at Cowpens, accompanied by Lt. Col. Henry (Light Horse Harry) Lee of the Continental Army, was moving west of Ninety-Six with the intention of keeping British troops in Augusta from reinforcing the British at Ninety-Six. Now, with a recovered Clarke in the field, he, as well as Pickens and Lee, all were focused on taking Augusta.

Learning that the British are moving gifts for the Indians toward Fort Galphin, Clarke moved his troops to intercept the goods. Fort Galphin was situated on the Savannah River between Savannah and Augusta, twelve miles below Augusta, at Beech Island. It was a distribution point and boats laden with gifts and supplies for the Indians were moving toward it. Although Clarke failed to capture the boats, his presence in the area prompted Lt. Col. Brown to send two companies of his King's Rangers from Fort Cornwallis in Augusta, to Fort Galphin to prevent it falling into Clarke's hands. This greatly reduced the strength of Brown's command in Augusta at a time when General Andrew Pickens and Lt. Col. Henry Lee were moving toward that post with the intention of driving the British out of the area.

Clarke laid siege to Fort Galphin with little success until a company of Lee's Legion joined him. The mounted Legion hid in the area and Clarke and his men attacked the fort, then feigned a retreat. The troops in the fort, thinking they had the Patriots on the run, left the fort to follow and finish off Clarke. Lee's mounted rode into the fort and overwhelmed the few soldiers who had been left to protect it. The British suffered 4 killed and 180 taken prisoner. Since the majority of the prisoners were Provincial, full-time, trained soldiers, it was a serious loss for the British. (O'Kelley, 2006, Vol. 3:243-245).

The skirmishes in the backcountry, as well as defeats such as King's Mountain, Blackstock's and Cowpens, had inflicted many casualties on the British forces. Now General Greene was back in South Carolina with his Continental Army and had moved to siege Ninety-Six.

The company from Lee's Legion and Elijah Clarke's militia moved from Fort Galphin to Augusta where General Andrew Pickens and Lt. Col. Lee were preparing to attack. (Rauch, 2006:32-56). The British had built two forts in Augusta to protect their troops and the Indian trade: Fort Grierson which was the fortified home of Col. Grierson, a local Tory, and Fort Cornwallis, a stronger and more conventional fortification. Col. Grierson commanded his post, and Lt. Col. Thomas Brown commanded Fort Cornwallis. The two forts were situated on the river with a ravine and rough terrain between them. The forts no longer exist but a marker for Fort Grierson is on the fire station on Reynolds Street in downtown Augusta, The marker for Fort Cornwallis is on the property of St. Paul's Church in Augusta.

Brown understood the danger of his situation. He had detached two companies of his King's Rangers which had been lost at Fort Galphin. Also, Ninety-Six was surrounded by General Greene's Continental Army so the British post there could not send troops to Augusta. Lt. Col Brown was not unaware of the sentiment against him, and that the Georgians with the Patriot forces were looking for revenge. Although British officers often held the militia in contempt, Clarke's militia was a cause for special concern. In addition to his corps of Wilkes County experienced and battle savvy veterans, Clarke's force included Major James Jackson who had been Pickens's adjutant major at Cowpens. Clarke's men, as well as the South Carolina militia under General Andrew Pickens, and the Continentals commanded by Lt. Col. Lee, comprised a force to be reckoned with and Lt. Col. Brown understood that. He sent for his Indian allies to come to his aid and about 300 came.

The Patriots first launched an attack on Fort Grierson in which Col. Grierson commanded local Tory militia. When he saw the determined Patriots advancing with axes to cut

Plaque Marking Site of Fort Grierson
Augusta, Georgia

away his stockade, he attempted to retreat to Fort Cornwallis which was close by. During the attack the Patriots killed thirty of the British and took forty-five prisoners.

As soon as Fort Grierson was captured, the Patriots lay siege to Fort Cornwallis. Although Brown had been called to surrender, he refused citing the presence of Elijah Clarke's 'rabble' as an excuse. Evidently he considered militia as unmilitary and would not surrender as long as they were in the Patriot force.

Needing to reduce Fort Cornwallis with artillery, the Patriots built a tower, filled the bottom with rocks for stability, and mounted a cannon, a six-pounder, which they had taken at Fort Grierson. With the elevated cannon, they were able to bombard Fort Cornwallis and disable the fort's artillery. Brown withstood the cannonade for a time by having his troops dig into the earth of the fort's walls for protection but it was of little use. On 6 June 1781 Lt. Col. Brown surrendered. (Rauch, 2006:44).

Site of Fort Cornwallis at
St. Paul's Church
Augusta, Georgia

Prisoners found inside Fort Cornwallis included men from Wilkes County who had been taken when Clarke attacked Augusta in May of 1780. Brown had hanged thirteen but those whom Brown had not hanged had been held hostage and those who survived were in horrible condition.

Jesse Gordon of Wilkes County was one of the prisoners. His pension application indicates extensive service during the Revolution and that he fought with the Wilkes County Militia at Carr's Fort and Kettle Creek and was involved at Clarke's earlier attack on Augusta. After that battle he was one of twenty-one of the settlers in Wilkes County who had been taken prisoner and interred in irons at Fort Cornwallis. (Gordon, 1833). He reported that he was released in June by Lt. Col. Lee.

Clarke's Wilkes County Militia was bent on revenge for those who had been hanged and those who had been mistreated. Naturally, Lt. Col. (Burn Foot) Brown was the target. General Pickens, recognizing that Brown was a prisoner of war, was determined to turn him over to the British in Savannah under parole. The prisoner was entrusted to Lee's Continentals to safely transfer the prisoner.

The Georgians were deprived of an opportunity to treat Brown to 'Georgia parole,' but they were not the only men who wanted Brown dead. Captain Tarleton Brown, of Andrew Pickens's South Carolina militia, related in his diary:

Brown had been such a desperate fellow, there existed great anxiety to kill him; but as he came under capitulation, we had no opportunity to do so at this time, but I determined to do so on his way down the river. I took a few brave fellows, and slipped down the river to carry into execution my determination, but he made his escape, through the shades of night, in a small canoe. (Tarleton Brown, p. 26)

Brown was turned over to the British as a paroled officer, but Col. Grierson was not so fortunate. The wounded officer was shot by a mounted rifleman who fired into his prison cell. It was widely believed that the Georgians were responsible, and the marker at the site states that he was killed by a Georgia rifleman. However, the Georgians were not the only men seeking revenge. O'Kelley suggests that there was no scarcity of men seeking revenge on the British in Augusta. On the assault on Fort Grierson, an officer of Lee's Legion, Major Pinketham Eaton, was wounded in the thigh. As he lay on the field, a Tory killed him with Eaton's own sword. An early North Carolina historian, David Schenck, makes the same point that the death of Grierson was the consequence of Eaton's death while a prisoner. He quotes a portion of a letter from a Colonel John Armstrong:

I have the disagreeable news to inform you of the death of Major Eaton. He was wounded at Augusta, taken prisoner and surrendered up his sword, and was afterwards put to death with his own sword. This I have by a letter from Captain Yarborough. (Schenck, 1889:419).

Captain Yarborough is listed as an officer serving under Major Eaton in the North Carolina Regiment. (Schenck, 1889:395).

Georgia historians, Edwin Cashin and Steven Rauch, have documented that Georgian James Alexander killed Grierson in retaliation for abuse of Alexander's elderly father after the first siege of Augusta.

The execution of Col. Grierson was condemned by both Major General Greene and Brigadier General Andrew Pickens. At a time when both were trying to bring a conclusion to the hostilities in the backcountry, the violence was continuing.

Finally—Chapter 14

With the British forts at Augusta leveled and the defenders captured, General Pickens and Lt. Col. Lee moved their troops and prisoners back across the Savannah. They joined Major General Nathanael Greene in his siege of Ninety-Six. (Dunkerly & Williams, 2006). Col. Clarke and Lt. Col. Jackson did not join them. There was much to be done in Georgia.

Now promoted to Lt. Col., James Jackson with Georgia militia moved toward Savannah. There was no possibility of that small group attacking the British stronghold, but the presence of Patriot militia in the area would discourage any attempt at stationing British troops at Augusta again. Also, the Patriot presence made it difficult for the Indians to move supplies or reinforcements to the British. The plantations along the coast supplied rice to feed the British at Savannah and became targets of the Patriots.

Col. Elijah Clarke took his militia back into Wilkes County to their devastated settlements. There was a continued threat to the settlers who returned in the person of Lt. Col. Thomas Waters. (Davis, 2006, **Waters**, 20-22). Waters, a Tory officer, commanded Georgia Loyalist militia and Indians. Also riding with him were white men who dressed as Indians, referred to as 'white savages.' Waters had been one of the original settlers in Wilkes County but, after he threw in his lot with the British, he had meted out terrible atrocities against his former neighbors. Clarke blamed him for the massacre of the settlers who had been left behind during the exodus from the area in October of 1780. Many of the prisoners had been turned over to the Indians to be tortured and killed. Now Lt. Col. Brown was gone from the area, but with Waters still free there would be no safety in Wilkes County.

Elijah Clarke and his young son returned to their family and settled at the abandoned plantation of Thomas Waters. Later the government in Georgia would confiscate that property and award it to Clarke for his war service.

As Jackson and Clarke moved back into Georgia, General Andrew Pickens and Lt. Col. Lee and their troops joined Major General Nathanael Greene in the siege of Ninety-Six. The siege was the longest siege in the Revolutionary War. It began on 22 May 1781 and ended 19 June when a relief column of British soldiers from Charleston arrived. General Greene, now outnumbered, moved away from Ninety-Six. He had failed to take the fort but had accomplished his intention of forcing the British out of the territory. The British destroyed the fortifications, burned the town and evacuated their troops as well as many of the local Tories. (Dunkerly & Williams, 2006:59).

In the north, the armies went into winter camp and hostilities ceased for a time. That had not been true in the south but the heat and humidity of the summer of 1781 brought misery to friend and foe alike. General Greene marched his army to the High Hills of the Santee (a plateau near present-day Sumter, South Carolina,) while the British Army was posted close to the Santee River. The wet winter had caused flooding along all the rivers, and men in both armies suffered from malaria and camp fever.

Mounted Continentals under the command of Lt. Col. Henry Lee and Lt. Col. William Washington campaigned in the low country to counter British troop movements. Militia under General Thomas Sumter and General Francis Marion used their mounted troops to annoy the enemy and interrupt the enemy's supplies.

Although the British had been pushed from their posts in the back country, the area was not pacified and Tory militia rode under the command of David Fanning and William

(Bloody Bill) Cunningham attacking Patriot militia. The level of violence kept escalating as local rivalries erupted and long-term grievances were revenged.

As General Greene rested his army he called for reinforcement for his next movement to push the British out of the Santee River area. In addition to the militia of General Andrew Pickens and General Francis Marion, he expected about one hundred fifty Georgians to join him at the High Hills. The Georgian militia did not respond although a few Georgians were among Andrew Pickens's militia. The situation in Georgia required constant monitoring. The trip would have taken the Georgians through the hostile Tory territory in the Ninety-Six district. Also, the distance required was long and the weather was brutal for men and horses and the smallpox had drained the physical resources of the survivors of that epidemic. The situation with the Indians was deteriorating. The decision the Georgians made was a wise one as circumstances would soon prove.

General Nathanael Greene's army engaged the British force at Eutaw Springs 8 September 1781. Although the British claimed the victory, it is still disputed today. (Swager, 2006: 135-143). The first day's action was a draw and when Greene returned the second day, the British were retreating. Again, Greene had accomplished his mission as the British moved their troops into Charleston.

On 19 October 1781, Lord Cornwallis surrendered his army to General George Washington and Count Rochambeau at Yorktown. The British Southern Strategy had been a failure and a costly one at that.

Although many people believe that the war ended with Yorktown, it was not the case. It would take almost two more years before the hostilities were concluded and, in the meantime, there were bloody and brutal encounters between the British supporters, the Loyalist or Tory militia, and the Patriots. Nowhere was the conflict more bitterly fought than in Georgia and South Carolina. Had the Georgian militia not been protecting their state, the results could have been catastrophic.

On 2 November 1781, Lt. Col. James Jackson, now commanding Georgia State Troops, intercepted a British patrol at Ogeechee River Ferry and scattered the enemy. (O'Kelley, 2006, Vol. 3: 381-383).

Clarke and his Wilkes County Militia were not idle. Indians who refused to make peace were attacked in Wilkes County on 6 November 1781 and killed: forty Indians and 2 white men. Also among the forty prisoners taken were more white men dressed as Indians. Clarke's men burned the villages and hundreds of bushels of corn and provisions. Pursuing the enemy, Clarke's men found food stores which the Indians had concealed and destroyed them. (O'Kelley, 2006, Vol. 3:384).

Tory leader, Lt. Col. William 'Bloody Bill' Cunningham had been pursued by his enemies and took refuge with the Cherokees. When he had gathered a sufficient force he returned to the fight. On 7 December 1781, Cunningham's men captured a convoy of wagons and took the Patriot patrol prisoner. They turned the prisoners over to the Indians who accompanied Cunningham to be tortured and killed. One of the men taken was John Pickens, the brother of General Andrew Pickens. Because of his relationship to the famous Patriot, he was targeted for gruesome torture and was burned alive. Before the war was over, the Cherokee nation would suffer retribution at the hands of Andrew Pickens. (O'Kelley, 2006, Vol. 3:405).

At the beginning of 1782, the British troops were confined to Charleston Neck and the fort at Savannah. However, their Loyalist militia and Indian allies were still in the field. A change in the government in England meant that the war would no longer be pursued and the British troops would be withdrawn as soon as negotiations could be concluded. However, there would be considerable bloodshed before that could be accomplished.

Major General Anthony Wayne had been sent by the Continental Congress to establish a civilian government in Georgia. (Harrington, 2006). South Carolina's legislature was already established in Jacksonboro on the Edisto River. Lt. Col. James Jackson was authorized to raise troops which were referred to as Georgia Legion. Patriot Governor Martin of Georgia offered leniency to former Loyalists who would now pledge their allegiance to the new government and many accepted the offer.

Naval operations along the Georgia and Carolina coast served to keep the British troops short of food and ammunition. However, the destruction of rice fields to keep the food out of the hands of the British, also caused a great scarcity for the civilian population. Patriot troops on the move were hard pressed to find food as the British destroyed everything as they moved.

While Wayne and Jackson focused their attention on Savannah, Elijah Clarke and his men moved across the Savannah River to join Andrew Pickens in South Carolina. Cherokee warriors had been joined by Tories such as William (Bloody Bill) Cunningham; Pickens had been ordered to patrol the Cherokee boundary in late 1781.

In March of 1782, Pickens set out with his South Carolina militia and Georgia militia to punish the Indians who had tortured and killed his brother. The force moved through the territory burning villages, destroying everything encountered. Forty Indians were killed and forty prisoners taken. The remaining Indians fled when the Patriots set fire to the canebrake. (O'Kelley, 2006, Vol. 4:38-39).

Meanwhile, General Wayne was determined to drive all the British from their outposts into the city of Savannah and that had been accomplished without much difficulty. Without troops to storm the fort at Savannah, he attempted to lure the British commander, Brigadier General Alured Clarke, to engage Wayne's troops in the field. General Clarke declined to leave the safety of the fort and called on his Indian allies for support.

Lt. Col. Thomas Brown, who had been turned over to the British on parole after his capture at Augusta, was once again in the field commanding his King's Rangers and he expected the arrival of his Creek allies. Brown sent a patrol out to the Altahama River to look for the Creeks. A detachment of Georgians with Wayne's Army discovered the patrol and drove them back. (Harrington, 2006).

On 12 May 1782, Lt. Col. James Jackson discovered a large detachment of Brown's men at Harris Bridge on the Ogeechee River. General Wayne joined Jackson and they attacked the British troops, killing forty and taking 18 prisoners. Brown escaped into the swamp and made his way back to Savannah. Wayne followed the fleeing enemy to Savannah but could not entice the British to leave the fort.

On 24 May 1782, a band of Indians, led by a British officer, attacked Wayne's camp killing 6 of the Pennsylvania Continentals and wounding eight. Twenty Indians were killed in the skirmish.

On 23 June 1782, a group of Creeks on their way to join the British at Savannah, made a surprise attack on Wayne's force at Ebenezer. When Wayne led a cavalry charge the Indians fled, leaving behind their pack horses. Eighteen Indians were dead and fourteen prisoners were taken. Wayne ordered the Indians shot. He had learned about 'Georgia parole.' (O'Kelley, 2006, Vol. 4: 67-68).

On 11 July 1782, the British evacuated Savannah. Lt. Col. James Jackson and his Georgia Legion accepted the surrender from General Alured Clarke. The British soldiers were shipped to Charleston or New York where they would eventually be shipped back to England. Provincial troops, who were Americans from New York, New Jersey and vicinity, shipped to the Islands or Nova Scotia. Lt. Col. Thomas Brown was among the departing troops and he, with most of his force, ended up in the British-held Islands of the Caribbean. However, he encouraged the Indians he had left behind to continue their attacks on the settlers insisting it was the white settlers in the back country, not the British, who were their enemies.

Hugh McCall, in his History of Georgia, writes that Savannah had been occupied for three years, six months and thirteen days, and the destruction in the state was enormous. The British took with them over seven thousand people, three thousand of them were British regulars and Loyalists, five hundred women and children, three hundred Indians and five thousand slaves. McCall estimates that three-fourths of the slaves owned by Georgians were taken by the British. Possibly half of the wealth of Georgia had been destroyed in the war.

However, the war was not over. One Tory officer who was conspicuously absent from the departing troops was Lt. Col. Thomas Waters. He still inhabited the mountainous regions of Georgia where he enlisted disaffected Indians and renegades to plunder and murder.

Georgians waited for the inevitable. In September 1782, Waters attacked. General Andrew Pickens and Colonel Elijah Clarke mustered 414 militia and rode into Cherokee country. With an insufficient supply of ammunition, Pickens ordered his men not to shoot women, children or any Indian who did not pose a threat. After taking women, children and a few men prisoner, he sent the men to their chief with the message that the quarrel was with the white men who commanded them, not with the Indians themselves. Pickens promised they would not continue to advance if the Indians returned their prisoners and turned over the white men. Otherwise Pickens would burn their villages. The chiefs agreed that they would turn over Waters and his men if Pickens would not attack the villages. They surrendered six of Waters's men and promised to capture Waters and turn him over to Pickens and Clarke. When Waters realized he no longer had the protection of the Indians, he made his escape to British Florida. (O'Kelley, 2006, Vol. 4: 89-90).

On 17 October 1782, an agreement was made ending the Cherokee War in which the Indians gave up the land between the Chattahochee and Savannah Rivers. The treaty was finalized in May 1783.

On 14 December 1782, the British had evacuated Charleston taking the last of their military with them. Five hundred ships were needed to take the British Army, Loyalists, their property including slaves, from South Carolina. Now, the two wars, The War for American Independence and the Cherokee Wars, were finally over. Although McCall estimated that half of the wealth of Georgia was gone, there is no way to count the deaths, or assess the pain, that the Americans in general, and the Georgians in particular, had suffered.

What of the men of Wilkes County? The heroes of Kettle Creek? Did any part of the country suffer more than the inhabitants of Wilkes County? Possibly not.

With the British gone and the Cherokee War ended, the Wilkes County Militia could look to the future. Those who survived had to start over. Their homes had been burned, family members killed, and part of some families still scattered. Everything left behind had been stolen or destroyed.

However, the men whose ancestors had moved from Scotland to Ireland, who had suffered religious persecution, who had made the harrowing trip to this continent, and who had migrated down the Wagon Road to this new frontier, would show the same determination in peace as they had in war.

They would rebuild!

The Aftermath

On 4 February 1783 Great Britain announced that cessation of hostilities against the former colonies. The war was over but it would take months of negotiations before the Second Treaty of Paris was signed on 3 September 1783. Now, the men who had led the fight for independence in the back country would work to rebuild their homes and their states.

General Andrew Pickens

Andrew Pickens returned to the Long Cane area and built a home called Hopewell which stands today on the property of Clemson University. He was elected a representative to the South Carolina Legislature and served as representative from his district in Congress.

Pickens believed that Indians and the settlers could live peacefully in the area and his efforts to facilitate this gained him the trust and respect of the Indians. Twice Pickens was commissioned, first by President Washington and later by President Jefferson, to negotiate treaties and to establish boundaries. The Treaty of Hopewell was signed at his home.

In his later years, Pickens moved further into the back country and built a home at Tamassee, close to the site of his Ring Fight of years before. He died there in 1817 and is buried at the Old Stone Church cemetery in Clemson. Pickens Counties in Georgia and South Carolina are named for Andrew Pickens.

Although Pickens had received a sword for his command at Cowpens, had been commissioned a general in South Carolina and had assisted two presidents, his modest headstone reflects the humility of character:

Andrew Pickens's Gravestone
Old Stone Church, Clemson, South Carolina

Elijah Clarke

Although Andrew Pickens believed that the white settlers could live in peace with the Indians, Elijah Clarke spent the remainder of his life in an effort to confiscate more Indian land for the State of Georgia.

Elijah Clarke was illiterate which was not unusual for men of his time. However, his son, John, who had accompanied him in the struggle for independence, was sent to university and given the best education a young man of the time could acquire. John became a governor of Georgia.

A grateful state gifted to Clarke the confiscated property of Loyalist Thomas Waters and Elijah and his wife, Hannah, spent the remainder of their lives there. They were buried on their property but when the Savannah River was dammed to make the lake which is known as Clark Hill (notice the state dropped the 'e'), the graves were moved to a fitting site on the shore of the lake. At Elijah Clark State Park Elijah and his wife were buried with a fitting memorial. The park includes a cabin where living historians relate the stories of the early life of the settlers of Wilkes County.

The property also includes the home site of John Dooly and a memorial marker is placed at Dooly Springs.

Every year on the second week-end of February, the Georgia Society, Sons of the American Revolution, celebrate the Battle of Kettle Creek with a moving ceremony at the site of the battle which is ten miles from Washington, Georgia, off State Route 44. The program on Saturday afternoon is open to the public and free of charge. Wreaths and flags are presented by chapters of Sons of the American Revolution, Daughters of the American Revolution, Children of the American Revolution, as well as other historic organizations and descendents of men who fought in the battle.

On Sunday morning, another ceremony takes place at the gravesite of Elijah Clarke at the Elijah Clark State Park. These events are fitting tributes to the heroes of Kettle Creek.

Elijah and Hannah Clarke Tombstone
Elijah Clark State Park

APPENDIX I

The Monument

From: Rauch, Steven J. **Kettle Creek Battlefield Bicentennial Marker Erected in 1979.** Southern Campaigns of the American Revolution, Vol. 3, No. 2.1. Camden, SC. Used with permission.

Entrance to Kettle Creek Battle Site

The Monument

The marker pictured here was erected in 1979 to observe the Bicentennial of the Battle of Kettle Creek. It was designed and researched by the Washington-Wilkes Historical Foundation, Dr. Turner Bryson, President, and The Kettle Creek Chapter of the Daughters of the American Revolution, Mrs. John Singleton, Regent.

THE PATRIOTS WHOSE NAMES APPEAR ON THIS MARKER ARE THOSE WHO HAVE BEEN PROVED TO HAVE PARTICIPATED IN THE BATTLE OF KETTLE CREEK ON FEBRUARY 14, 1779.

Wilkes County Regiments, Georgia Patriot Militia
(140 men)

Col. John Dooley, Commanding
Lt. Col. Elijah Clarke
Major Burwell Smith
Capt. Alexander Autry
Capt. John Cunningham
Capt. William Freeman
Capt. Daniel Gunnels
Capt. James Little*
Capt. Joseph Nail, Sr.
Lt, William Black
Ensign Joseph Nail, Jr.
Archibald Simpson
David H. Thurman
Micajah Williamson
Isham Burke
Owen Fluker
Micajah Brooks
Charles Gent
Jesse Gordon
William Hammett*
James Hays
Jesse Hooper

David Madden
Benijah Noridyke
Peter Strozier
Benjamin Thompson
John Webb
Nathan Smith

* Wounded at Kettle Creek

Upper Ninety-Six Regiment, South Carolina Patriot Militia (200 men)

Col. Andrew Pickens, Commanding
Capt. Andrew Hamilton
Capt. Robert Anderson
Capt. James McCall
Capt. Joseph Pickens
Capt. Thomas Weems
Capt. Levi Casy
Lt. Joseph Calhoun
Lt. Alexander Ramsey
Lt. Samuel Roseman
Lt. Thomas Shanklin
Lt. Joseph Wardlaw
Thomas Langdon MD
William Anderson
John Bird
Willis Breezily
William Buchanon
Alexander Patterson
Samuel Reed
John Trimble
Patrick Cain
Francis Carlisle*
William Carruthers
Thomas Cofer
Edward Doyle

Thomas Hamilton
John Harris*
William Hutton
Andrew Liddle
John Loard
James Luckie
William Luckie, Jr.
John McAdams
John McAlphin
Joseph McClusky
Elijah Moore
Samuel Moore
Richard Posey
William Speer
William Turk

* Wounded at Kettle Creek

Additional South Carolinians from The Auditor General Account Book, 1778-1780, South Carolina Department of Archives and History.

William Adams
Alexander Aaron
Robert Anderson
William Baskins
John Beard
David Beard
Robert Bell
John Bole
John Buchanan
William Brown
Willis Breazeale
George Crawford
George Deardon
John Calhoun
James Cane

James Caldwell
James Calvert
William Carothers
Daniel Carmichael
Alexander Chevas
Thomas Cofer
Cosby
Capt. John Cowan
Thomas Coyle

Additions to the Memorial Marker

John Thompson
William Downs
Nathan Barnett
Austin Webb
John Milner
John Barnett
William Thompson
Samuel Whatley, Private
David Hollomon
Edmund Butler
Absolom Davis

Based on work by Robert Scott Davis. Used with permission.

The research to determine the participants at The Battle of Kettle Creek is ongoing.

APPENDIX II

Roster of Georgians at King's Mountain

I am indebted to Brett Osborne of the Georgia Refugees for the following:

Sources are:
Moss, B.G. *The Patriots at Kings Mountain.*
Bailey, J. D. *Commanders at Kings Mountain.*
Dunkerly, R. M. *Kings Mountain Walking Tour Guide.*
O'Kelley, P. *Nothing but Blood and Slaughter. Vol. 2*

Muster rolls and Memoirs

Major William Candler (Moss) Commander
Captain Stephen Johnson (Moss) Commander
Captain Patrick (Paddy) Carr (Moss)
John Black (Moss)
John Crawford (Moss)
Timothy Duick (Moss)
Ebenezer Fain (Moss)
Captain William Hammett (Moss)
Captain Richard Heard (Moss)
James Patterson (Moss)
John Rainey (Dunkerly & Bailey) Died of wounds.
Peter Strozier (Moss)
John Torrence
Dennis Trammel –Capt.? (Moss)
Peter Trammel (Moss)

The website of the Georgia Society of the Sons of the American Revolution has additional names for whom the search for documentation is ongoing.

TIME LINE FOR GEORGIA

1663   The Carolina Charter gave to the Lords Proprietors territory which included Georgia.

1721   British established Fort King George at Darien to protect against the Spanish.

1732   June. New colony of Georgia was chartered.

       July. General Oglethorpe appointed leader of new Colony of Georgia.

       November. The ship *Anne* sailed from England to the New World.

1733   13 January. *Anne* landed in Charleston.

       12 February. Landed at Yamacraw Bluff. Savannah was established.

1736   Plots laid out for the fort and town of Augusta.

1738   September Gen. Oglethorpe's regiment arrived.

1739   Fall. Stono Slave Rebellion.

       October. War with Spain declared.

1742   July. The Battle of Bloody Marsh. McCall reports: Spanish 5000 soldiers Oglethorpe 650 soldiers

1743   July. Oglethorpe left Georgia not to return.

1752   Trustees surrendered their charter and Georgia became a royal colony.

1758   Sunbury established on the Medway River, protected by a fort, later Fort Morris.

1773   Transfer of Indian lands: "Ceded lands."

1774   Indian attacks on the settlers in the Ceded Lands.

1776   2 March. Battle of the Rice Barges, Savannah.

28 June. British attacked Sullivan's Island in South Carolina but were repulsed.

30 June. Indian attacks from Georgia to Virginia. Elijah Clarke wounded in skirmish with Indians.

1777   Treaty with Indians signed at DeWitt's Corner.

1778   November. British attack on Sunbury. "Come and Take It!"

29 December. British capture Savannah.

1779   31 January. British occupy Augusta.

14 February. **Battle of Kettle Creek.**

March. Battle of Brier Creek.

September. French-American attack on Savannah.

1780   Siege of Charleston. City falls 12 May. Pickens and Dooly take paroles.

12 July. Dunlap attacks at Cedar Springs.

13 July. Georgians take Gowen's Old Fort.

14 July. Dunlap attacks at Earle's Ford.

15 July. British evacuate Fort Prince.

30 July. Patriots capture Fort Thicketty.

8 August. Battle at Cedar Springs, Wofford's Iron Works, Clarke wounded.

18 August. Battle of Musgrove's Mill.

14-18 September. First Siege of Augusta.

September (end). Beginning of Exodus of Georgia Refugees.

7 October. Battle of King's Mountain.

9 November. Battle of Fishdam Ford.

20 November. Battle at Blackstock's.

12 December. Battle at Long Cane. Clarke seriously wounded.

25 December. Pickens reports to Daniel Morgan.

30 December. Battle at Hammond's Store.

1781   17 January. Battle of Cowpens.

17 January – 14 February. Race to the Dan River.

25 February. Pyle's Hacking.

6 March. Battle of Wetzel's Mill. (Pickens and the Georgians return home.)

21 March. Battle at Beattie's Mill. Dunlap killed. Smallpox in Wilkes County Militia. McCall dies.

May. Clarke attacks Fort Galphin.

June. Forts Grierson and Cornwallis in Augusta fall to the Patriots.

19 June. British evacuate Ninety-Six.

8 September. Battle of Eutaw Springs.

19 October. Lord Cornwallis surrenders at Yorktown.

6 November. Indians attack Wilkes County.

7 December. Andrew Pickens's brother is captured and killed by Indians.

1782   March. Andrew Pickens retaliates against Indians.

12 May. Attack at Harris Bridge in Georgia.

24 May. Indians attack Patriot camp in Georgia.

23 June. Attack at Ebenezer.

11 July. British evacuate Savannah.

September. Waters and Indians attack settlers. Pickens and Clarke campaign against Indians.

17 October. Indians agree to end hostilities.

14 December. British evacuate Charleston.

1783   May. Treaty is signed with Indians ending the Cherokee Wars.

3 September. The Treaty of Paris was signed, ending The War for American Independence.

PERSONS OF INTEREST

Terminology used in the following:

Those who fought for the British are identified, where possible, as:

British Regular: These soldiers were part of England's profession army. The units were recruited and trained in Great Britain and then moved to North America to fight.

British Provincial: Not having a sufficiently large force of Regulars, the British organized units in America of persons loyal to the King. They were equipped, armed, trained and paid by the British and were full-time soldiers.

Loyalist (Tory) Militia: These men were citizen-soldiers, local settlers who would muster and fight when needed.

Those who fought for the Americans are identified as:

Continental: Men who were enlisted in the Continental Army of General George Washington. Their enlistments were usually for three years. This was the full-time army authorized by Congress.

Patriot (Whig) Militia: These were citizen-soldiers who fought for independence. They were local settlers who would muster and fight when needed.

There were also **State Troops**, who were recruited for longer service than militia, who don't figure prominently in this narrative.

There will be some discrepancies in the ranks as officers were promoted over time. For example, Andrew Pickens was a colonel when he fought at Kettle Creek in 1779, but was a general when he defeated the British at Augusta in 1781.

Capt. Robert Anderson. (Patriot Militia) A member of Pickens's Brigade who fought at Kettle Creek: later fought at King's Mountain, Musgrove's Mill, Cowpens and Eutaw Springs.

General John Ashe. (Patriot) North Carolinian who was defeated at Brier Creek. Taken prisoner by the British, he suffered from smallpox and died in October, 1781.

General Benedict Arnold. (Traitor) Early in the war Arnold was a competent and courageous general. Later he changed allegiance and, by the end of the war, was commanding British troops in Virginia.

Lt. Col. (James? John?) Boyd. (British Provincial) Moved south with the British and commanded the Loyalist forces at Kettle Creek where he was killed.

Lt. Col. Thomas Brown. (British Provincial) Recruited a provincial force from Loyalists in Florda called The King's Rangers. His feet were disfigured when he was tarred and feather early in the war and he was thereafter known as 'Burn Foot' Brown. He was a bitter opponent of the Wilkes County Militia maintaining a vendetta against Elijah Clarke.

Maj. William Candler. (Patriot Militia) Georgian in Wilkes County Militia who commanded the Georgians at King's Mountain.

Lt. Col. Archibald Campbell. (British Regular) Commanded the initial successful assault on Savannah and then commissioned officers to recruit Loyalists in the back country of South Carolina and Georgia.

Brigadier General Alured Clarke. (British Regular) Succeeded General Prevost as commander at Savannah. Surrendered that city to the Americans on 11 July 1782.

John Clark. (Patriot Militia) Son of Elijah Clarke and, as a captain in the Wilkes County Militia, fought under his father's command. Possibly was at King's Mountain. After the war he became Governor of Georgia.

Col. Elijah Clarke. (Patriot Militia) A Georgian who was possibly the most capable and committed Patriot commander in the campaign. He commanded the Wilkes County Militia. In his memoirs, Col. Isaac Shelby reported that, at Musgrove's Mill, he had stopped to watch Clarke fight. Georgia's Clarke County and Elijah Clark State Park are named for Elijah Clarke.

Sir Henry Clinton. (British Regular) Commanded the British military forces in America.

Lord Charles Cornwallis. (British Regular) Although technically he was under the command of Clinton, he conducted the war in the south as if he had no superior.

Lt. Col. John Cruger. (British Provincial) He came south with DeLancy's Brigade, a provincial unit recruited in New York. He commanded the British garrison at Ninety-Six and campaigned along the Savannah River.

Maj. John Cunningham. (Patriot Militia) A Georgian with the Wilkes County Militia, he fought at Kettle Creek. At Cowpens, he commanded the Georgia militia, and then moved with Andrew Pickens in the 'Race to the Dan'.

Lt. Col. William Cunningham. (Loyalist Militia) Recruited as a commander of Loyalist militia, he was called 'Bloody Bill' for his practice of slaying his prisoners. He was subordinate to Major Patrick Ferguson who used

Cunningham's brutality to intimidate the Patriots in the backcountry.

Col. John Dooly. (Patriot Militia) A Georgian who commanded the Wilkes County Militia before taking a parole. While under the protection of the British as a paroled officer, he was brutally murdered. Georgia's Dooly County is named for John Dooly.

Capt. James Dunlap. (British Provincial) Came south with Patrick Ferguson and fought under that officer's command. A favorite tactic was to attack sleeping soldiers at night and to kill them with swords or bayonets. He seemed obsessed with destroying Elijah Clarke. He died, possibly murdered, after his defeat by Clarke and McCall at Beattie's Mill.

David Fanning. (Loyalist Militia) He, like Cunningham, fought under the authority of Patrick Ferguson and, like Cunningham, was considered a brutal adversary. He was forced to leave the country at the end of the war.

Maj. Patrick Ferguson. (British Regular) A soldier of the 71st Regiment of Foot (Frazer's Highlanders), he recruited a cadre of Provincials in South Carolina in an attempt to conquer and control the backcountry. He died at King's Mountain.

Col. Benjamin Few. (Patriot Militia) A Georgian who commanded Georgia militia. Occasionally his unit campaigned with the Wilkes County Militia.

Major General Horatio Gates. (Continental Commander) A general who had performed well in the north, had been defeated at the Battle of Camden. He was re-assigned in late 1780.

Major General Nathanael Greene. (Continental Commander) He replaced General Gates in late 1780 to become the commander of the Southern Continental Army. His strategy would reclaim the Carolinas and Georgia which was territory the British had occupied but could not hold. Georgia gave Greene a plantation on the Savannah River in thanks for his services. He died there and is buried in Savannah. Georgia's Greene County is named for Nathanael Greene.

Maj. John Hamilton. (British Provincial) At the time of Kettle Creek he was recruiting for Loyalist militia. However, he would later recruit and command the Royal North Carolina Regiment. .

Col. LeRoy Hammond. (Patriot Militia) South Carolinian who fought in the backcountry of the Carolinas and Georgia.

Nancy Hart. Nancy and her husband, Benjamin, were early settlers in Wilkes County. She was a devout Patriot and a courageous fighter against Indians and Loyalists. Georgia's Hart County is named for Nancy.

Capt. Shadrick Inman. (Patriot Militia) Georgian belonging to the Wilkes County Militia. His conspicuous gallantry was instrumental in the Patriots winning the Battle at Musgrove's Mill where he was killed in the last stages of the battle.

Capt. Joshua Inman. (Patriot Militia) Georgian who commanded the pickets at Cowpens.

Lt. Col. Alexander Innes. (British Regular) Moved from the British Army Headquarters in New York to South Carolina where he organized the South Carolina Royalists. Leading the British Provincials at Musgrove's Mill he was seriously wounded.

Lt. Col. James Jackson. (Patriot Militia) Active with Georgia militia, he was brigade major (second in command to Pickens) of the militia at the Battle of Cowpens. He accompanied Pickens on the 'Race to the Dan.' Later he organized Georgia State Troops and occupied Savannah when the British evacuated it. He later became Governor of Georgia. Georgia's Jackson County is named for James Jackson.

Capt. Stephen Johnson. (Patriot Militia) A member of the Wilkes County Militia, he fought with the 30-member group of Georgians at King's Mountain.

Capt. John Jones. (Patriot Militia) A Georgian who led a company of about thirty men from Burke County into South Carolina. His men captured Gowen's Old Fort, but were attacked at Earle's Ford where Jones suffered eight saber wounds on the head. He turned the command of his men over to Elijah Clarke and they were absorbed into the Wilkes County Militia.

Lt. Col. Henry Lee. (Continental Officer) A flamboyant commander of Lee's Legion, he was known as Light Horse Harry. He joined Pickens and the Georgians in North Carolina, and at Augusta.

Major General Benjamin Lincoln. (Continental Commander) Lincoln commanded the Continental Army in the South until he was forced to surrender his troops at Charleston. Georgia's Lincoln County is named for General Lincoln.

General Francis Marion. (Continental Officer-Patriot Militia Commander) After the fall of Charleston, Marion, an officer in the Continental Army, took command of a militia force and campaigned against the British in the river systems of eastern South Carolina. He was known as the 'Swamp

Fox.' Georgia's Marion County is named for General Marion.

Governor Martin. (Georgia Governor) After Major General Anthony Wayne and Lt. Col. James Jackson secured the Georgia area, a civilian government was established to conduct the state affairs.

Capt. James McCall. (Patriot Militia) A South Carolinian who was closely connected to Andrew Pickens. Fought at Kettle Creek, Augusta, Long Cane and commanded the mounted militia at Cowpens. A veteran of 17 battles, he died of smallpox.

Col. Charles McDowell. (Patriot Militia) A North Carolinian who commanded the Carolina militia and was joined by Elijah Clarke and Isaac Shelby.

Col. Joseph McDowell. (Patriot Militia) Commanded the North Carolina skirmishers at the Battle of Cowpens.

Maj. Daniel McGirth. (Loyalist Militia) An officer who was campaigning in north Georgia at the time of the Battle of Kettle Creek.

Brigadier General Daniel Morgan. (Continental Officer) Although there are many instances of his conspicuous bravery, it is his victory at the Battle of Cowpens which is part of the story of the Georgians. Georgia's Morgan County is named for General Morgan.

Brigadier General William Moultrie. (Continental Officer) He commanded the South Carolina Continental Line and was captured when Charleston fell to the British in May 1780.

General James Edward Oglethorpe. (British General) Established the colony of Georgia, and promoted its settlement. Built forts to protect the area from the Spanish and withstood a Spanish attack at the Bloody Marsh, ending the Spanish threat to the southern colonies.

General Andrew Pickens. (Patriot Militia) Although Pickens had, at one time been a soldier with South Carolina troops, it is as an Indian fighter and a militia commander that he is most widely known. The commander at Kettle Creek, he would later take a parole. When that parole was violated he returned to action at Cowpens, 'the Race to the Dan,' Augusta, Ninety-Six and Eutaw Springs. Georgia's Pickens County is named for Andrew Pickens.

Major General Augustine Prevost. (British Regular) Commanded British troops in Georgia during most of the British occupation.

Lt. Col. John Mark Prevost. (British Regular) Campaigned in Georgia where he was instrumental in the defeat of the Americans at Brier Creek.

Col. John Sevier. (Patriot Militia) Commanded militia from western North Carolina which is now eastern Tennessee. He was one of the commanders at King's Mountain. Later, Sevier was the first Governor of Tennessee.

Col. Isaac Shelby. (Patriot Militia) Also commanded militia from western North Carolina which is now eastern Tennessee. His men, known as Overmountain Men ("the yelling boys") fought at Musgrove's Mill and King's Mountain. Served as a senator in the United States Senate after the war.

Maj. William Spurgen. (Loyalist Militia) Subordinate officer who served under Lt. Col. Boyd at the battle of Kettle Creek.

Col. John Stark. (Patriot Militia) Commanded the New England militia which defeated part of Burgoyne's British Army at the Battle of Bennington.

General Thomas Sumter. (Patriot Militia) A South Carolinian, Sumter was active in that state, mostly west of the Santee River. His militia units were drawn from across the state and often included Georgia units as at Blackstock's. After the war he represented the state in the United States Senate. Georgia's Sumter County is named for General Sumter.

Major Samuel Taylor. (Patriot Militia) Part of Thomas Sumter's force, he joined Elijah Clarke and James McCall in their attack on Augusta.

Col. John Twiggs. (Patriot Militia) A Georgian who commanded Georgia militia and assumed command after General Sumter was wounded at Blackstock's. Georgia's Twiggs County is named for Colonel Twiggs.

Lord Tryon. (Royal Governor) As governor of North Carolina at the time of the Regulator Movement, his troops defeated the Regulators at the Battle of Alamance. The brutal treatment of the defeated Regulators caused many settlers to move farther south.

General George Washington. (Continental Commander) The commander of the Continental Army. After the Revolutionary War he became the first president of the new nation. Georgia's Washington County is named for President Washington.

Lt. Col. William Washington. (Continental Officer) A commander of Virginia cavalry who fought at Hammond's store and Cowpens. A second cousin of George Washington.

Lt. Col. Thomas Waters. (Loyalist Militia) An early settler in Wilkes County, he supported the British and with Loyalist militia and Indians conducted a campaign of terror.

Major General Anthony Wayne. (Continental Commander) He was sent to Georgia after the defeat of the British at Yorktown to establish a civilian government. His Pennsylvania Continentals were involved in confining the British to Savannah and in warding off Indian attacks. Georgia's Wayne County is named for General Wayne.

Col. James Williams. (Patriot Militia) Commander of the Little River Militia, he fought at Musgrove's Mill. He was mortally wounded at King's Mountain.

Lt. Col. Micajah Williamson. (Patriot Militia) A member of the Wilkes County Militia, he fought at Kettle Creek. When Elijah Clarke was ill with smallpox, he turned the command of the Wilkes County Militia over to Williamson.

General Andrew Williamson. (Patriot Militia) A commander of the South Carolina Militia, Williamson fought at Brier Creek and at Savannah. When Charleston fell, he took a parole. He was considered a traitor at the time but recent research suggests he might have been a spy for the Patriots while a a prisoner.

Governor James Wright. (Royal Governor) Georgia's governor in the period leading up to, and during the American Revolution.

References

Babits, L. (1998). *A Devil of a Whipping.* Chapel Hill, NC: The University of North Carolina Press.

Babits, L. (1993). *Cowpens Battlefield: A Walking Guide.* Johnson City, TN:The Overmountain Press.

Baker, T. E. (1981). *Another Such Victory.* Eastern National Press.

Blethen, H.T. & C.W. Wood Jr. (1999). *From Ulster to Carolina.* Raleigh, NC: North Carolina Department of Cultural Resources.

Brown, T. (1999). *The Memoirs of Tarleton Brown*. (Prepared by Charles I. Bushnell in 1862). Barnwell County Museum and Historical Board.

Buchanan, J. (1997). *The Road to Guilford Courthouse.* New York: John Wiley & Son, Inc.

Cashin, E. (1996). *The Story of Augusta.* Spartanburg, SC: The Reprint Company.

Cashin, E. (1999). *The King's Ranger.* New York: Fordham University Press.

Coleman, K. (1978). *Georgia History in Outline.* Athens, GA: The University of Georgia Press.

Coleman, K. (1991). *Georgia in the American Revolution.* In K. Coleman (Ed.), *A History of Georgia* (pp.71-88). Athens, GA: The University of Georgia Press.

Dameron, J. D. (2003) *King's Mountain.* Cambridge, MA: Da Capo Press.

Davis, R. S. (2006) *The Battle of Kettle Creek. Southern Campaigns of the American Revolution. Vol. 3 No. 2.1* 30-37.

Davis, R. S. (2006). *Colonel Thomas Waters: Georgia Loyalist. Southern Campaigns of the American Revolution, Vol. 3 No. 9:* 20-22.

Davis, R. S. (2007). *Elijah Clarke:Georgia's Partisan Titan. Southern Campaigns of the American Revolution. Vol. 4 No. 1,* 38-40.

Draper, L. C. (1881). *King's Mountain and Its Heroes.* Johnson City, TN: The Overmountain Press.

Dunkerly, R. M. (2006). *Prelude to Guilford Courthouse. Southern Campaigns of the American Revolution, Vol. 3 No. 3,* 34-43.

Dunkerly, R. M. & Williams, E. K. (2006). *Old Ninety-Six: A History and Guide.* Charleston, SC: The History Press.

Eller, E. F. (1900). *The Women of the American Revolution.* Philadelphia, PA: George W. Jacobs & Co.

Gordon, Jesse. (1833) Pension application of Jesse Gordon. Transcribed by W. T. Graves.

Graves, W. T. (2002). *James Williams:An American Patriot in the Carolina Backcountry.* Lincoln, NE: Writers Club Press.

Hagist, D. N. (2004). *A British Soldier's Story: Roger Lamb's Narrative of the American Revolution.* Baraboo, WI: Ballindallock Press.

Harrington, H. T. (2006). *"The Enemy are Hounded": Gen. "Mad" Anthony Wayne's 1782 Savannah Campaign. Southern Campaigns of the American Revolution. Vol. 3 No. 4*, 32-36.

Hays, L. (1946). *Hero of the Hornet's Nest: A Biography of Elijah Clark, 1733-1799.* New York: The Hobson Book Press.

Higginbotham, D. (1961). *Daniel Morgan: Revolutionary Rifleman.* Chapel Hill, NC: The University of North Carolina Press.

Hope, W. (2003). *The Spartanburg Area in the American Revolution.* Spartanburg, SC: Altman Printing.

Lambert, R. (1987). *South Carolina Loyalists in the American Revolution.* Columbia, SC: The University of South Carolina Press.

Leyburn, J. G. (1962). *The Scotch-Irish: A Social History.* Chapel Hill: The University of North Carolina Press.

McCall, H. (1909). *The History of Georgia; Containing Brief Sketches of the Most Remarkable Events Up To the Present Day (1784).* Atlanta, GA: Cherokee Publishing Company.

McGee, L. F. (2005). *"The better order of men...": Hammond's Store and Fort Williams. Southern Campaigns of the American Revolution Vol. 2 No. 12,* 14-21.

McKenzie, R. (1787). *Strictures on Lt. Col. Tarleton's History Of the Campaigns of 1780 and 1781, in The Southern Provinces of North America.* London.

Murray, S. (1998). *The Honor of Command.* Bennington, VT: Images of the Past.

O'Kelley, P. (2004). *Nothing but Blood and Slaughter: The Revolutionary War in the Carolinas, Volume One: 1771-1779.* Booklocker.com. Inc.

O'Kelley, P. (2004). *Nothing but Blood and Slaughter: The Revolutionary War in the Carolinas, Volume Two: 1780.* Booklocker.com, Inc.

O'Kelley, P. (2005). *Nothing but Blood and Slaughter: The Revolutionary War in the Carolinas, Volume Three: 1781.* Booklocker.com, Inc.

O'Kelley, P. (2005). *Nothing but Blood and Slaughter: The Revolutionary War in the Carolinas, Volume Four: 1782.* Booklocker.com, Inc.

Rauch, S. J. ((2006). *"A Judicious and Gallant Defense": The Second Siege of Augusta, Georgia. Southern Campaigns of the American Revolution, Vol. 3, Nos. 6-7-8.1,* 32-56.

Rauch, S. J. (2005). *"An Ill-timed and Premature Insurrection": the First Siege at Augusta, Georgia September 14-18, 1780. Southern Campaigns of the American Revolution. Vol. 2 No. 9,* 1-17.

Rouse, Parke, Jr. (1995) *The Great Wagon Road.* Richmond, VA: The Dietz Press.

Scoggins, M. (2005), *The Day It Rained Militia.* Charleston, SC: The History Press.

References

Shelby, Isaac (1814). *Isaac Shelby's Account of his Exploits During the Revolutionary War.* Transcribed and annotated by William T. Graves. In *Southern Campaigns of the Revolutionary War, Vol. 2 No. 3*, March 2005.

Spaulding, P. (1991). *Colonial Period.* In K. Coleman (Ed.), *A History of Georgia* (pp. 9-70). Athens, GA: The University of Georgia Press.

Stokesbury, J. L. (1991). *A Short History of the American Revolution.* New York: William Morrow and Co.

Swager, C. R. (2002). *Come to the Cow Pens!* Spartanburg, SC: Hub City Writers Project.

Swager, C. R. (2006). *The Valiant Died : The Battle of Eutaw Springs, September 8, 1781.* Westminster, MD: Heritage Books.

Tarleton, B. (1787). *A History of the Campaigns of 1780 and 1781, in the Southern Provinces of North America.* Reprinted in Cranbury, NJ: The Scholar's Bookshelf, 2005.

Index

Index

Index